The Principles

THE PRINCIPLES

*HAPPINESS AND INTEGRITY
IN LOVE, HEALTH, PARENTING, AND
WORK*

Patrick Moore

12th street jam books
www.12thstreetjam.com

12th street jam books

a division of

12th street jam

1311 1/2 12th Street

Santa Monica, CA 90401

www.12thstreetjam.com

THE PRINCIPLES:

HAPPINESS AND INTEGRITY

IN LOVE, HEALTH, PARENTING, AND WORK

ISBN 978-0-6151-4055-1

First Edition

Printed in the United States of America

12th street jam would like to thank the following people for their support on this project:

First and foremost, we are grateful to Deanna Brown, Rachel Friedlander, Margie Gilmore, and Matt Hanover of Yahoo! for their belief in this work and for helping us to reach a worldwide audience.

Thanks also to Cyrus Krohn, Harold Goings, and Jeff Markus at Yahoo! for their assistance and Kathy Watt for her generosity. Michael Bourret at Dystel & Goderich Literary Management also proved himself a loyal friend during this process. And George Snyder provided careful editing and thoughtful suggestions. Finally, Joaquin Navarro and Cameron Whiteman provided support on the home front. We are grateful to all of you.

Contents

Introduction to The Principles

I think you want to be happy. We all do. Our spiritual instinct is to be happy. Why then are millions of people desperately unhappy even when so many of their dreams have come true and they are surrounded by the things they want? *The Principles* will give you tools to take responsibility for your problems, change your life, and find happiness.

You will have to be willing to leave self-pity behind to go on this journey. You will need to drop the word "victim" from your vocabulary. And you will especially need to be more honest than you've ever been before. In exchange, I can absolutely guarantee you that your life will transform and that problems with love, work, and health will fall away. I have good reason to be confident that you will get results. The concepts that are described here have been at the heart of all the world's great belief systems, from ancient

1

religions to modern self-realization systems. This book simply presents you a roadmap for utilizing them.

Ultimately, *The Principles* can be reduced to two basic ideas:

- *You play a part in each and every one of your problems. If you stop playing the victim, you have the opportunity to change your life.*
- *If you want to change your basic character, you will need to develop and maintain some kind of spiritual connection. But you do not need to be religious.*

If that sounds vague, you needn't worry. *The Principles* uses powerful, universal ideas but gives you practical tools for implementing them in your life.

These ideas aren't new. You'll recognize them from the world's great religions and philosophies. Some readers will find they resonate with 12-step work that they've done, perhaps working with a sponsor in Alcoholics Anonymous. Parts of this process will be familiar to people who have gone to Catholic confession or worked with a sponsor in Alcoholics Anonymous. However, even if you aren't Catholic and able to recite the Eight Beatitudes or the Seven Spiritual Works of Mercy, or you've never been to an AA meeting, you've probably

2

heard of the Seven Deadly Sins and the Ten
Commandments. If you're a Buddhist you know the
Four Noble Truths. Yoga students may have studied
Patanjali's 195 sutras. But, in the end, numerology isn't
the issue; it simply doesn't matter what your religious or
spiritual background is because the Principles are broad
enough to help anyone.

Although I am not a moral authority, I can
promise you one thing based on my personal
experience: *The following nine Principles work.* They
have transformed my life and the lives of millions of
other people, regardless of their individual belief
systems. For the first time, in this book, the nine
Principles are gathered together and presented not only
as ideas but as practical, daily exercises for solving
your problems.

So what are these Principles and where do they come
from?

SURRENDER is an idea that most of us avoid at
all costs, but it is the cornerstone of many spiritual belief
systems. Think of the sense of acceptance that is at
the heart of Buddhism; that idea is very close to what I
mean by surrender. Surrender as a Principle
encourages us to stop uselessly fighting the world and,

3

instead, focus on improving our own spiritual lives. Those who attend 12-step programs are familiar with the sense of relief that comes with surrender. Yoga practitioners advocate surrendering to the body's limitations even while working toward a higher spiritual and physical idea. So get rid of the idea that Surrender is a pessimistic idea. In *The Principles*, it is the key to hope and change.

The word FAITH sends chills down the spines of those of us who are too cool and cynical to believe that there is any operating system running this crazy world. *The Principles* will show you how spiritual faith is possible even if you rebel against organized religion. *The Principles* embraces every belief system. Ultimately, if you can take a walk in nature or remember someone who once loved you without reservation, you are as capable of having faith as someone who is deeply religious. But *The Principles* does not in any way reject religion and this work will do nothing but strengthen your existing beliefs.

RESPONSIBILITY is a word that gets thrown around a lot even though we may have trouble coming up with examples of it in modern society. Even some religions don't seem very fond of responsibility. But as an ideal, responsibility is at the heart of civic life in

4

America. I have a responsibility to myself as well as the community I live in. Our elected officials have a responsibility to represent those who elect them. Even if politicians and neighbors don't often embrace responsibility, it doesn't mean that you can't.

HONESTY is at the heart of powerful rituals such as Catholic confession. (We're not talking about telling the cashier when you get too much money back...although that's nice too.) In *The Principles*, Honesty is an exercise in sharing your faults with another human being and relinquishing some of the deep, dark secrets that weigh down your life.

HUMILITY is an amazing quality that has been admired throughout the ages, but it is difficult to define. However, it plays a central role in many religious and spiritual communities. Religious orders display modesty and respect as an indicator of humility and use it as a tool to get closer to their deity. Those in recovery from drugs and alcohol find humility in accepting that they are no longer in charge of their lives. As you begin to consider this Principle later in the book, remember that Humility is very different from *humiliation*. The point of this process is not to humiliate you by pointing out your bad behaviors but to give you the humility that comes

5

with accepting that you are just another member of the human race – no better and no worse.

FORGIVENESS is the touchstone of Christianity in its purest form. Christians believe that God forgives them and absolves them of their sins. We see Forgiveness play out in daily life when extraordinary people forgive those who have harmed them, knowing that continuing to be a victim will only bring more pain. And, of course, 12-step programs embrace the idea of asking for Forgiveness and forgiving others as a path to reentering life.

We are all told about PERSEVERANCE growing up. It's why "quitter" is such a nasty insult. But we seldom think about what Perseverance means on a practical level. Certainly, many of the world's people have persevered through wars, famines, and poverty. In the developed world, Perseverance has a different but just as important meaning. How often do we make great progress in our lives, only to get lazy or full of ourselves? If we Persevere, we accept that we will inevitably backslide and need to work on ourselves some more if we want to continue to grow as spiritual beings.

Often mistaken for religion, SPIRITUALITY is individual and private. In *The Principles*, Spirituality

6

never means proselytizing to or judging others. My spiritual beliefs are my own. My God (or Higher Power) only works for me. You will find your own Spirituality, perfectly suited to you, on this journey. Whatever brings you a sense of connection and real safety is spiritual. Note that I will use different terms throughout this book – God, Higher Power, Nature – to name the being or force different people believe in. For those opposed to religion, the word God will make you uncomfortable. For those who are church members, the idea of believing in a Higher Power or Nature might seem blasphemous. I would encourage you to keep an open mind and remember that *The Principles* is simply a roadmap to your own spiritual destination.

From AmeriCorps to missionaries to those who feed the poor, HELPING OTHERS is practiced as a tool for self-esteem and spiritual growth. So often, though, we are not spiritually fit ourselves and cannot be of maximum usefulness when we try to Help Others. In *The Principles*, Helping Others comes at the end of a process that ensures we can selflessly give of ourselves and gain true self-worth.

You may have heard of ideals such as honesty, faith, and forgiveness back in Sunday school but, let's get

7

real, it's unlikely that you see them as part of your daily life. As much as we're taught to live by the Golden Rule, most of us plow through life on a quest to succeed and leave quite a bit of wreckage in our wake.

Rather than integrating these ideals into our daily lives, many of us indulge in their dark and destructive opposites. We actually enjoy our bad behavior, even though it often comes with a terrible price tag. Who doesn't love to judge their best friend, wallow in hatred for their screaming boss, and blame their parents for the mess of adulthood? Forget self-awareness and taking responsibility...bring on the greed, jealousy, and selfishness!

The only problem is that, when the lights go out and we're alone, we see ourselves for who we've become. Despite the houses and cars and big screen TVs, most of us are pretty damn unhappy most of the time. *The Principles* offers a practical way to take responsibility for your mistakes, clean them up, and live daily life with integrity and the simple goal of feeling better about yourself.

The problem you face may seem huge and life-long. Or it may be a simple irritation that's come up lately. Either way, *The Principles* can provide guidance, solace...and hope.

8

The work I will suggest you do in *The Principles* boils down to owning up to whatever your problem is, praying for some help, taking responsibility, seeing what parts of your personality created the problem, cleaning up your messes, keeping the faith and helping other people. Believe it or not, it's all pretty easy.

How to Use This Book

You can use *The Principles* on your own but it will be even more effective with a friend, a book club, a spiritual advisor, a therapist, or buddies on-line. (You can visit www.12thstreetjam.com to find a range of forums and other tools.) One of the most effective ways for you to stop repeating the same bad behavior that got you in whatever mess you're in (and you must be in one or you wouldn't be reading this) is to stop keeping it a secret. A secret is a terrible thing because it reinforces the idea that you're a bad person; that no one else has made so many mistakes; that you're alone.

But if you use *The Principles* with another person, even a stranger, you'll find that you're life may be messy...but it's not all that unique. There's no need to be ashamed anymore.

9

And I need to ask you one last thing when using this book. Read these pages in order and discover each Principle sequentially. I know this is a lot to ask in an on-demand world but I want you to get the greatest benefit possible from the effort you put into this process.

For example, the last Principle, Helping Others, is a great activity no matter when you try it. However, you and the person you are helping will get so much more out of it if you have already Surrendered and taken Responsibility for your problems. The same is true of Forgiveness. It's always great to forgive and be forgiven, but it is so much more powerful if you've done the work of having Faith and practicing Honesty.

I know that your life will improve if you do the work outlined in this book. So don't shortchange yourself by skipping important parts of the process. That would be like baking a cake with only some of the ingredients!

Cast of Characters:

Our problems range from mundane and silly to really horrible. However, no matter what the rest of the world thinks, they are *our* troubles and we think about them non-stop, all day long, and then dream about them when we go to sleep. (Ever have a dream about trying to find something, or running from some nameless, faceless enemy?)

Most of our problems fall into the broad categories of love, work, parenting, and health. The characters that appear in every chapter of *The Principles* collectively represent this range of problems. Although they are fictionalized composites, their problems are drawn from real people I have known and wished that I could help. Here are the characters who will illustrate for you how *The Principles* can work in real life:

Helen (Dating) – Helen may be in her thirties but, when it comes to love, she has the emotional maturity of a teenager. She's a lot of fun but she's a brat. Helen loves the bad boys but seems surprised when they don't call for a second date, much less express any interest in relationships. Helen has been "looking for love in all the wrong places" for a long time now and the search has gotten painful enough that she's actually ready to make some changes in her dating strategies.

Tom (Work) – Tom drives 90 minutes each way to and from work on the highways that stretch from the

11

suburbs of Dallas to its corporate towers downtown. When he gets to work, he faces off each day with a boss who alternately berates Tom and then tries to be his friend. Tom fears that he is going to explode in a fit of road rage one day.

Marlene (Marriage and Parenting) – Marlene thought being a fulltime mom was her dream so she quit her job as a successful lawyer in a small town. She was happy for several years after her daughter was born but now she and her husband want to have another child – a boy – and they can't seem to get pregnant. Their sex life, which was already precarious, is now entirely focused on procreation rather than recreation.

Bernie (Dating) – Bernie is a wildly successful television producer in Hollywood but he can't find love. However, he can find a long line of beautiful young men, mostly actors, who want to use him. Although Bernie is rich and powerful now, he is still wounded by memories of being called "faggot" throughout his childhood.

Ashley (Weight Loss/Health) – From the time she was a child, Ashley has had a wealth of excuses and

12

resentments about her weight. Ashley's entire family is obese and her mother's cooking tends toward Tater-Tot casseroles and Kraft macaroni and cheese. Ashley often moans, "I was cursed from the gate!" Now 28, Ashley is beginning to see that her weight is both an excuse and an obstacle, keeping her from meeting a man and enjoying life to the fullest.

Tool Kit:

Although using *The Principles* isn't complicated, you'll need a few simple tools that might be new to you. You'll find these tools at the end of the book, along with some resources for more serious problems that require professional help.

One of the most useful tools I've ever been given is the **Feelings List**. Earlier in life, if you asked me how I felt, I would probably have said "good" or "fine" or "angry" or "worried." It didn't get much deeper than that.

I don't think I'm unique in not having been raised to be aware of my feelings. Most adults are completely out of touch with their feelings. We may say that we're afraid or angry but, if we really think about it, we're just as likely to be feeling greedy or superior. If you're ready to change by surrendering to your problems, you'll stop

moaning about them and then saying, "But I'm fine."
Instead, use your Feelings List and tell someone how
you really feel.

To use your "feelings list," state your problem
out loud and then read through the list, saying each
feeling that applies. Don't look for what you think you
feel. Just let your eyes go down each column and see
what jumps out. You may be surprised at the extent of
your feelings and how little you've explored them. Once
you see how badly you feel about your problem,
perhaps you'll be willing to surrender to a solution.

Another useful took included in this book is a list of what
I like to call **Broken Behaviors**. Religious people term
these sins, 12-steppers call them character defects.
For me, they are bad habits that were once useful
(confidence, for example) but became destructive.
They are broken. Yet I still continued to use them and
create a terrible mess, both for myself and others.

Need an example of how a good behavior
becomes broken? Think of your youth when you felt
confident about something. As the years go by and the
disappointments and fears pile up, that confidence often
becomes *arrogance*. You could say the same thing

14

about *ambition* becoming *greed*, or *relaxation* becoming *laziness*.

The reason to look at these Broken Behaviors is to change them. They are creating your problems.

At the end of each chapter, you will find a **Mantra** pertaining to the Principle you are reading about. A mantra is a short phrase you repeat aloud or in your head over and over as a reminder to keep up your resolve. And, finally, I've included some **Prayers** that I've written specifically for this book. Each prayer relates to one of *The Principles*.

As someone who is not particularly religious, I always felt distant from prayers, even ones that I liked. With their elaborate language and heavy associations, they just didn't bring the comfort and connection I craved. So I've endeavored to write some modern, no-nonsense prayers that I hope will be helpful to you.

Action:
We're not going to get too heavy in this book but, on the other hand, I want to be clear that this is about getting off your butt and doing something. Only action brings change. And the good news is that you *can* change!

15

CHAPTER ONE
SURRENDER

Remember when your kid brother would sit on you and twist your arm? Hurt, right? What did you yell when you couldn't stand it anymore? "I give up! Uncle! I surrender!" Unless he was in a particularly sadistic mood, he probably let you go and you felt relieved.

I'm pretty inflexible (in every sense) and, when my yoga teacher instructs me to take the dreaded Pigeon Position, I break into an immediate sweat. With one leg folded under me, my other leg stuck out behind, and the weight of my body pressing down onto my hip, I desperately try to breathe through the pain. My moaning must be rather alarming because the instructor often comes over, brushes her hand over my head and whispers, "Surrender." Somehow the pain lessens.

In Western culture, surrender is a very dirty word. When we face a problem, particularly in America,

16

we force our way through the pain and just keep moving. But using the force of our will is very different than having any real power over a troubling situation. When it comes to our most vexing problems, the ones that keep us awake at night, we are mostly helpless.

We also feel somehow that we have to stay positive if we are ever going to improve our lives. When faced with the worst, most intractable problem, we smile bravely and proclaim, "But it's not so bad! I'll get through this!"

Although it may seem strange to you, I would suggest you take the opposite tact. Surrender. You've fought this war long enough and you have lost. All your strength, self-reliance, and positive thinking have gotten you absolutely nowhere in dealing with love, parenting, health, and career problems. In fact, you've made it worse.

The word surrender is often associated with war, specifically defeat. But what would happen if neither side in a battle ever surrendered? The war would go on forever. Indeed, we need only turn on the television to see many examples of battles that have raged on for decade after decade because each side is convinced that that they are right. But the truth is that both sides in the battle suffer. Both lose lives. Normal life is

17

impossible. Nothing exists but the battle. If one side surrendered, at least the possibility of change would exist. Even when surrender means defeat, it can be hopeful.

So I propose you take a leap of faith. Ironically, what seems like weakness now as you surrender will lead to real power and real change in the very near future.

For those of you who hate the idea of surrender, let me suggest an even more disturbing idea. Just think of yourself as a dog!

I am a great believer in taking lessons from the animal world, which does not suffer from the terrible burden of ego and other broken behaviors. I once heard a famous dog trainer explain how surrender and submission can bring peace to animals. This man works extensively with aggressive dogs, such as pit bulls. When he encounters a problem dog, his goal is to get the dog to surrender by rolling over and exposing its stomach: the most vulnerable position for an animal.

Dogs who are at risk of losing their homes, even being destroyed because of aggressive behavior are forced, sometimes easily and sometimes with great difficulty, into laying on their backs even while they

18

continue to snap and snarl. Gradually they become quiet. The trainer strokes and reassures them that they are safe, even in this defenseless position. When dogs surrender in this way, they change almost immediately. They become a part of the pack. They are not alone.

Would you say that these dogs have been humiliated? Would it have been a better choice for them to continue to destroy their lives through aggression (usually fueled by fear) or to surrender to a power greater than themselves? Rather than being humiliated, these dogs appear to be happy. I hope you will forgive me for saying so, but I think we have a lot to learn from these dogs who learn that surrender is a path to belonging.

Fortunately, you will not require an animal trainer, just some simple tools and a healthy dose of honesty. But first, let's meet our characters and watch them surrender. Remember, these are not real people, although they are based on real people I know. Each character represents an area of your life – dating, work, marriage, parenting, and health – where you can utilize *The Principles*. The characters will help you identify your problem and see concrete examples of how The Principles can be used.

19

In each profile of Surrender, you will see the following:

- The person admits that they have a problem they cannot fix.
- The person uses their Feelings List (see the Tool Kit at the end of this book) to get honest about how this problem has been making them feel.
- The person surrenders and becomes willing to try something new.

Helen (*Dating*)

Helen still thinks of herself as a "girl" even though she's well into her thirties. With her dark mane of hair and trim figure (always shown to its best advantage in designer clothes), she doesn't have a hard time attracting men; it's just that none of them seem to be interested in a relationship. Recently, Helen relocated to Los Angeles from New York because "all the guys in New York are jerks."

However, the change of scenery hasn't improved Helen's love life and she is mystified that the LA bad boys she dates don't seem to be the marrying type. When confronted with the fact that bikers and Hollywood agents aren't known for their relationship abilities, Helen gets defensive, "Look, if there isn't any chemistry, what's the point?"

Helen is also very resentful toward her mother who, along with a hefty allowance, provides non-stop nagging about settling down. It's not that her mother can't afford to help but the financial assistance comes with unsolicited advice that only makes Helen feel more guilty and frustrated.

When Helen hits the clubs in Hollywood, the velvet ropes part and free drinks abound. Surrounded by the beautiful people, though, Helen feels alone, knowing that she's still dating the same bad boys she liked in High School. Ironically, the good news is that she is totally powerless over her choices in love. The even better news is that there is hope if she surrenders and gets real about how afraid she is to be loved.

Helen Surrenders to her Dating Problems

Helen had sex with a Malibu surfer last Saturday night and has spent the entire week waiting for him to call. Having now left three voicemails (one more than she usually allows herself), she knows that he won't call back. Even if he does call, Helen finds herself asking if

21

she really wants to spend her weekends wearing a wetsuit and paddling around Santa Monica Bay.

Although the surfer didn't call, Helen's mom did. Using the Surrender Worksheet (at the end of this chapter) Helen had just written, "I surrender to the fact I might never find a man." When mom asked how she was doing, Helen's first impulse was to scream, "Fine! Why do you always ask me that?" Instead, Helen burst into tears and had the humility to tell her mother, whom she's always considered her worst critic, exactly how broken down and lonely she feels.

When her mother heard Helen say that she felt ashamed, infantile, incomplete, and lonely, it was clear that something had changed. (Helen has been perusing the "Feelings List" provided in *The Principles* Tool Kit section.) Helen's mother told her daughter how much she loved her, and that she deserved better than the men she had been dating.

This week when Helen and her friends get together, they're going to try something different. Instead of moaning about what jerks men are and putting on a brave face, they're going to get real about what it feels like to still be making bad choices while looking for love.

22

<u>Tom</u> (*Work*)

Tom is a study in barely controlled rage. After he spends more than an hour on the Houston freeways tailgating and flashing his headlights at the "schmucks" on the road, he arrives at work to face his boss, who is literally standing at the front door, to see if Tom is late…again.

Tom's boss, whose favorite mode of communication is an all-out meltdown scream fest, has a taste for breaking down any employee who he perceives to be lazy or insubordinate. Although Tom stuffs his anger as far down his gut as possible, there is no mistaking the curl of his lip. As for laziness, Tom replies, "Maybe I could work harder but with a boss like mine who'd want to?"

Night after night, when Tom gets home to suburbia, he just sits and stares at TV for hours. His head buzzes with imaginary arguments long after he goes to bed. And, after violent dreams, Tom wakes up to start all over again.

Before he has to break out the defibrillator, Tom needs to surrender to the fact that he cannot change his boss. He can't control the other drivers on the road, their cell phones, the perpetual traffic jams, and the

23

effects of his own anger. If Tom sat down in his cubicle one day and took some time off from his rage and frustration, he might begin to see that the only thing he can change is himself.

Tom Surrenders to his Work Problems
The other night, Tom pulled into his suburban garage and just sat there, staring straight ahead. Earlier, during his lunch break, he'd read about surrender in *The Principles*. It infuriated him; the last thing he wanted to do was surrender to his jerk of a boss.

Then Tom started thinking about what his life was really like. All day, every day, he was furious. It wasn't like he could hide it. His friends had dwindled to a few other guys as bitter as he was. His wife had left several years ago, not able to deal with his continual foul mood.

As he got out of the car, Tom thought about all the people he had glared at during the drive home. It wasn't that they had just irritated him. No, he had *hated* every one of them. True, some of them were bad drivers, but most of them were just trying to get home after a hard day's work.   Tom's stomach ached.

Tom isn't' big on writing things down or using books but, standing in his kitchen that night, he

24

muttered, "I can't do this anymore." He glanced at the "Feelings List" and, of course, his eyes leapt to *angry*. But he also connected to *afraid*, *battered*, *caged*, *idiotic*, and *out of control*.

Tom surrendered. He was just too tired to fight anymore. He couldn't take one more day trying to change his boss and, more importantly, he didn't want to spend another day feeling the same way. He was surprised to hear himself say, "I give up." Things were about to change for Tom.

Marlene (*Marriage and Parenting*)
Marlene speaks in capitals. She's never just tired – she's completely and utterly FRIED. Her daughter just hit the terrible twos but she LOVES being a fulltime mom instead of billing hours as a corporate lawyer. She loves it SO much that Marlene and her husband want ANOTHER child, specifically a boy.

The problem ("PROB" as Marlene would say) is that they can't get pregnant again. Sex has become totally about procreation as opposed to recreation. Marlene is not one to give up though. She is not about to accept that she might not be able to have another child. Even in her small Midwestern town she has found a yoga class at the community college,

25

discovered mail-order herbal teas, and researched space age fertility treatments on the Internet.

Friends who suggest adoption are treated to a long lecture on the absolute importance of the blood bond. Marlene will brook no thought of those starving Siberian babies as she watches the sun glint off the silver framed portrait of her perfect, mini-me daughter.

Marlene has a secret though. She's totally miserable and can't really remember why having another child seemed so important. But now that she's talked for so long and so relentlessly about her pregnancy crusade, she's ashamed to admit she's increasingly unsure. Marlene needs to surrender to the reality that another child may not be her dream and work on enjoying the baby she already has.

Marlene Surrenders to Marriage and Parenting
A weird thing happened to Marlene the other day. Waiting in the pediatrician's office, she was reading *The Principles*. When she saw the word "surrender," she burst into tears.

Later that afternoon, Marlene put her daughter down for a nap and was enjoying a little fertility tea while reading more of *The Principles*. She looked at the

26

logo on the tea box – a mother cradling a child. She sobbed for an hour.

Marlene's ovulation cycle was at its height so that night she and her husband planned to "get to work." After putting their daughter to bed, they dutifully marched upstairs to the bedroom. Sitting on the bed, Marlene started weeping again and told her husband just how confused she was about having another child. He held her while she cried and told her that he understood.

Ironically, they made love that night like that hadn't in years.

The next day, Marlene sat with her "Feelings List" and thought about having another child. She kept looking for the word *hopeful* but seemed to be drawn back to *trapped*. When she thought that *rewarded* would apply, her eyes focused on *crazy*.

Marlene stood in the doorway of her daughter's room that day, watching the little girl play. She flipped through some of her old law books that had long been packed away. Finally, Marlene ran her hand over a brochure for yet another fertility treatment. She sighed, "I just don't know." Somehow, those words seemed hopeful instead of confusing to her.

27

<u>Bernie</u> (*Dating*)

Bernie seems to have everything as he walks through his mid-century-modern house in the Hollywood Hills surrounded by his art collection. Success came early for him in the television business and, at age fifty, his career continues to thrive in a business not known for longevity.

Yet, each night as he looks out at the lights of Los Angeles, Bernie is bone-crushingly lonely. His loneliness does not mean that he doesn't get any sex. Bernie has dated every hot, young actor in Los Angeles – gay, straight, or questioning. Bernie likes the young James Dean type: tragic although he doesn't know it yet.

Bernie doesn't think about the age difference between him and the "boys" he chases. He never considers that they might be using him. If they turn out to be drug addicts or messes, he thinks it's bad luck. Bernie just falls in love – totally and stupidly in love. Well, OK, "falls in lust" might be a better description.

It's time for Bernie to sit down in front of that gorgeous view, with those Emmys glittering on the shelf, and have a good long look at himself. Intelligent, charming, handsome, and filthy rich, Bernie hasn't had one real relationship in his life. He needs to surrender

28

to the fact that he chooses men who will never be able to love him.

Bernie Surrenders to his Dating Problems
Bernie thought that he'd conquered his emotions. After a debacle with a busboy (he'd never gone below the waiter level before) he'd been dating, Bernie told himself he was finished with love. "From now on," he thought, "the boys will just be beautiful possessions, rewards for my hard work, beautiful glittering things no different than a house, car, cell phone, or a painting."

To celebrate his new resolve, Bernie hosted a pool party. Most of the young men who came were actors and they flocked around him. Suddenly, they all started to look the same; their tans, rippling abs and blinding smiles were identical. Bernie felt a panic attack coming on and rushed into the den. Sitting there was a copy of *The Principles* he'd bought months before.

Flipping through the chapter on "Surrender," Bernie felt like he was drowning. He looked around the magnificent house. He glanced at his Cartier watch. He ran his hand through his expensively cut hair. Three words came out of his mouth: "*Shallow… superficial…sorry.*"

29

Bernie cancelled all of his appointments this morning. He is sitting in bed, looking out the window. Even though he didn't drink at the party, he feels hungover. The sun is shining and Los Angeles sprawls majestically below. But everything looks different. Nothing has changed…except Bernie.

Ashley (*Weight*)

With a laugh that sounds like a tinkling bell, a lively sense of humor, and a sweet nature, Ashley is adored by everyone and surrounded by a loving family. Why does she feel like a complete failure then? Because the only thing Ashley knows about herself is that she's fat.

For all of her sweetness, Ashley is starting to panic and develop a long list of resentments. Ashley often moans, "I was cursed from the gate!" And it's true that her entire family is obese and her mother's cooking tended toward recipes with lots of carbs, calories, sugar and lard.

Ashley says she's "too busy to exercise." But the truth is that she's embarrassed to go to the gym in her small hometown because everyone knows her. "There she goes again," she thinks people will whisper. And, because there are plenty of other overweight people in town, she doesn't feel much pressure to

30

change. But, at 28, it's been several years since she went on a date and she hasn't had a serious boyfriend since High School. With her biological clock ticking and loneliness closing in, Ashley has more or less decided that the situation is hopeless.

But hopeless is very different from being willing to change. Ashley needs to surrender to the idea that she is making herself miserable. In fact, her unhappiness has little to do with her weight. She can become thin but first she needs to look at the underlying reasons food seems so comforting to her.

Ashley Surrenders to Weight Problems

Ashley pulled a large, stuffed-crust pizza with pepperoni and pineapple out of the oven yesterday and plunged into one of her feeding frenzies. She was so upset all she could do was eat, and the more she ate the more upset she got.

If pushed, Ashley might have said she was lonely or disgusted with herself; she never delved deeper. "Upset is upset," she thought. Yet, she's been reading *The Principles* and decided to give the "Feelings List" a try.

With a mouthful of pizza, she mumbled, "I surrender to my weight problem. That makes me

31

feel…nothing." But words kept popping out at her from the Feelings List. *Agonized. Bitter.* She noticed that she was drumming her fingers on the tabletop by the time she got to *caged* and *condemned.* With *doomed* and *exhausted* she stood up. But it wasn't until she read the word *feminine* that she took the pizza and turned it into a projectile, flinging it at the wall.

Standing there, panting, she watched the pizza slide down the wall and thought about that word again. *Feminine.* Why did that make her so mad? Ashley's journey has begun.

To sum up about surrender…

So, kind of a drag, right? Not only do you have a problem, you've got to surrender to it. The thing is, you've already tried every possible solution to this problem - you think about it obsessively until your head hurts. In fact, it's gotten so bad that you've even resorted to visiting the dreaded Self-Help section in the bookstore. And this isn't a new problem. In fact, it's kind of a variation on every problem you've ever had.

I suspect that, although you talk about it incessantly, you've never really accepted how much this problem and other similar ones hurt. You've been so busy processing the problem in your head and your mouth that you've never let it sink into your heart so that you can really own it.

When you hear surrender, you hear failure. But guess what? You failed already. The war is over and you lost. Now, if you own up to how far down this problem has taken you, you can start to work your way back up.

But in the real world…people walk all over you if you just surrender. You roll over and expose your soft underbelly, you'll get hurt…won't you?

If this is a real crisis you're in, you can't get hurt much more. No matter how silly it might seem to the rest of the world, you're in pain. All of your efforts and will power haven't really made much of a difference. In fact, they've made it worse. What have you got to lose?

34

Surrender Worksheet on _____(problem).

Five ways my problem makes me feel (use Feelings List in the Tool Kit):

_____

_____

_____

_____

_____

Five ways I've lost my self-respect because of this problem:

_____

_____

_____

_____

_____

Ways I've tried to control the problem and failed:

_____

_____

_____

35

Tips on surrender

- Surrender doesn't mean you get to be lazy. It leads to taking action.
- There's a difference between force and power.
- There's a relief in being defeated – you can only go up.
- Don't minimize your problems. They're yours and they feel serious to you.
- Have a good cry. Admit it: your problem hurts.

Mantra

I surrender to _____ but am willing to change.

Tool – Feelings List

Most adults are completely out of touch with their feelings. We may say that we're *afraid* or *angry* but, if we really think about it, we're just as likely to be feeling *greedy* or *superior*. If you're ready to surrender to your problem, you need to find out how and what it's making you feel. You need to experience the depth of those feelings instead of glossing over them. This is part of surrendering

Stop using the word, "Fine." It's mostly a lie. When friends ask you how you are, really tell them. The Feelings List in the Tool Kit section at the end of *The Principles*, will help you get real about your emotions.

Don't be surprised if you have conflicting feelings at the same time. For example, it is completely natural, if you are going out on a date, to feel both *eager* and *terrified*. Once you are on the date, you might feel both *grateful* and *bored*. It is exactly these pairings of feelings that are most revealing. If I am *grateful* to go out with a person who might actually be interested in me, I might feel *bored* because I'm used to the excitement of someone glamorous but unavailable.

Don't worry. You're not going to spend the rest
of your life wandering around reading your feelings off a
piece of paper. But in the privacy of your home or with
a trusted friend, the Feelings List is a remarkable tool.
And eventually you will become more familiar with your
real emotions rather than just settling for *fine* or *good*.

To use your "feelings list," state your problem
out loud and then read through the list, saying each
feeling that applies. You may be surprised at the extent
of your feelings and how little you've explored them.
Once you see how badly you feel about your problem,
perhaps you'll be willing to surrender to a solution.

CHAPTER TWO
FAITH

Now that you've identified the feelings around your problem and surrendered, you can see that you have absolutely no control over whatever is making you crazy. So what do you do now that you have accepted the seriousness of your situation and have admitted what it feels like?

In times of crisis like this, along with a string of expletives, you've probably also whispered that secret little prayer, "Dear God, please help me." For most of us, particularly those of us who aren't religious, it's just a figure of speech. But what if we all had our own personal God (call it a Higher Power, as they do in 12-step programs, if that's easier) who could indeed help us when we are literally helpless? Might we start to feel some hope for the first time in years?

Once we've surrendered and stopped trying to control our problems, we have to make a leap of faith.

39

This doesn't necessarily entail a religious ceremony or a big revelation. Maybe you feel some peace in the world when you walk by the ocean or look up at the stars in the night sky. Whether or not you're religious, you know that the ocean is more powerful than you...just try stopping the waves. You know the expanse of night sky is bigger than you are...try willing the stars not to shine.

You can have an even more personal faith. Is there someone who loved you unconditionally earlier in life who has now passed on? Surely that person's spirit would want you to be happier than you are right now. They would want things to change. This idea of God has been particularly effective for me. Sometimes, I literally think of all the people who have loved me and are no longer here. I imagine them just standing around me. I know they would want me to change and make a better life for myself...with their help.

Whatever your God turns out to be, it should inspire a feeling of safety. In that frame of mind, we try to have faith that we are meant to be live life as a joyous adventure rather than the dreary rut if feels like to you right now. Our tired old strategies for defeating our demons haven't produced spectacular results, so really, what do we have to lose in having faith that some

40

greater being in the universe could figure out this problem. All we need to do is have faith and ask.

The majority of the world's religions (Christianity, Judaism, Islam) are monotheistic: they believe in one Supreme Being. In these belief systems, God seems to be such a huge, universal presence that it can be difficult to ask God for help with what may seem a mundane problem with work, love, or parenting. Although these problems may not be a matter of life and death, they can make us feel that life isn't really worth living. I think these are exactly the kinds of dilemmas where we need to utilize faith if we are to lead fulfilling happy lives.

Christianity, especially Catholicism and its derivative religions, has solved this problem by assigning certain saints to help people with practical challenges. For example, prayers to Saint Joseph are meant to help maintain a healthy marriage and Saint Monica can be counted on when my children disappoint me. The saints bring faith into the daily lives of believers.

Hindus believe in a range of manifestations of the Divine, each with domain over a certain part of life. Writers may be drawn to Ganesha, the elephant god

41

who wanted so badly to write that he broke off his tusk and used it as a quill. Those looking for prosperity and success at work might pray to Lakshmi, who sits on a lotus with her four hands extended. To ward off evil, other worshipers may turn to the blue-skinned Krishna.

So, for religious people, it should not be difficult to integrate faith into a program addressing their everyday problems. As for those who do not participate in organized religion, that does not mean faith is out of reach.

For example, Alcoholic Anonymous has a long tradition of encouraging agnostics to participate in a program that requires spiritual faith. Countless recovering alcoholics and addicts have found faith in one another, seeing that kindness and understanding to one another brought about a feeling of connectedness. And ultimately, that is the point of faith. Faith allows us to believe that we are not alone with our problems. When combined with action, faith can bring incredible change to our lives.

Now, listen, enough of the eye rolling. I don't care if you find God in a church or on the *Oprah Winfrey Show*. I don't care if you worship Jesus, Buddha, or Allah. The fact is that nothing else has worked, right? So you

42

might as well try a spiritual answer and have faith. Make your own God. You don't need mine for this to work, but I promise you this: faith has worked for me when nothing else did. I have witnessed it work for many others.

You've surrendered to the facts and feelings of your problem. It's a big problem. Why not try a big solution? What have you got to lose?

Faith and Dating (Helen)

Helen was never one for church but that doesn't mean she isn't spiritual. In fact, spirituality was one reason she moved to California from New York. There was something about nature, even in the big flat sprawl of Los Angeles, which Helen couldn't ignore. Whether it was the palm trees swaying in the wind, the snow-capped mountains ringing the sun-drenched city, or the constant call of the ocean, Helen sometimes had a sense of peace in nature.

It's been a week since Helen surrendered and really admitted to her mother and a couple of friends how she feels about her love life. For the first few days, she felt weepy and wiped-out. She'd taken long walks in big sunglasses with an Hermes scarf wrapped tightly over her head – "very Jackie O.," she thought. But she quickly got tired of the smeared mascara and self-pity.

A new thought came into her head late one afternoon as Helen stood on the Venice Pier, staring out at the golden ripples of the sun setting over the Pacific. She looked toward Malibu and, for a moment, stopped thinking about the surfer who never called her back. Instead, she thought, "I know there's something better out there for me."

44

That night, lying in bed, Helen looked at the photo of her father she kept on the nightstand. Although he'd died when she was only six, Helen remembered her dad vividly – how dashing he was, how he'd taught her to waltz with her little feet standing on top of his. If anyone had ever wanted her to be happy and loved, it was him. Tears slid down Helen's face, but they weren't entirely sad tears. Her whisper was barely audible in the quiet room, "Dad, please help me find the right person."

Faith and Work (Tom)

Tom tries to put everything back together when he loses it. "Sure," he thought, "I got kinda upset about work but it's no big deal."

He put away his Feelings List and the feelings that went along with his problems at work. For a week, he showed up early at work, forced a smile when other drivers cut him off, and ran as far as his legs would take him every night in the Texas heat. Then he dropped a bottle of wine on the kitchen floor one night, and put his fist through the wall.

So Tom has literally been trying to put things back together since he surrendered. He swept up the

45

broken bottle and patched the hole in the kitchen wall. But what about the hole in his gut?

Last Sunday, Tom went to church for the first time in years. Tom had gotten mad at God at some point. When his wife left him, when his career didn't work out, when...he had a long list of complaints toward God.

But Tom enjoyed the church service. Frankly, he didn't listen to the sermon very carefully. He just felt a sense of peace sitting there. Afterward, he even spoke to the priest, who he'd known for 20 years. The priest shook Tom's hand and asked Tom how he'd been. At first, Tom told the priest how great life was.

The priest smiled and nodded. "Now, how are you...really?"

Tom's face turned red as he stuttered, "Kinda lost. Angry. Work and stuff like that. I need some help."

Tom prayed with his priest the next day.

Faith and Parenting (Marlene)
The most precious moment in Marlene's day is bath time. When her daughter is in the tub, splashing happily and telling stories about her rubber duckies,

46

nothing seems wrong with the world. With the steamy windows and the quiet house, Marlene almost feels like she's in church instead of a second floor bathroom.

Since she surrendered to the fact that she really doesn't know if she wants another child, Marlene has felt oddly calm. When she was a practicing lawyer, she always thought that things needed resolution after a period of careful consideration. But Marlene has stopped thinking about a new baby. She has stopped thinking about her law career. Instead, she just waits for bath time.

One night, Marlene's daughter told her a story about the three rubber ducks bobbing around in the tub. "There's three…a mommie, a daddy, and me."

"Where are they going?" Marlene asked her daughter, who was intently building a castle out of the foamy remnants of Mr. Bubble. "Are they going to that castle?"

Marlene's daughter looked quizzically at her mother. "Oh no, Mommy. They're just gonna stay home and wait."

"Wait for what, baby?"

"Just wait. They don't need to go anywhere."

As Marlene sat and listened to her daughter splash and sing, she thought to herself, "Neither do I."

47

Faith and Dating (Bernie)

No one ever accused Bernie of not being interested in spirituality. When Madonna went to Kabbalah, Bernie followed. When Meg Ryan devoted herself to Siddha Yoga, so did Bernie. Yogis, psychics, sweat lodges...Bernie tried them all. Yet there was still a deep emptiness inside him.

The day that Bernie surrendered haunted him. He couldn't shake the feeling of sitting in his picture-perfect house, surrounded by picture-perfect men, and feeling more alone than he thought possible. Since then, Bernie has worked the same spirituality circuit he has been on for years. The activities are the same, but Bernie is different. Whereas before he went to his meditation session and yoga classes waiting for the hand of God to reach down and transform him, Bernie is now really seeking in the way of someone who has surrendered. He wants to change rather than *be* changed. He's willing.

Last weekend, Bernie went to a meditation retreat in the desert with a guru. It was very Hollywood and included lots of the usual hot guys Bernie saw regularly in LA. But Bernie wasn't so interested in them.

48

He was more interested in the sense of connection he felt.

On the last night of the retreat, all of the devotees sat in the night air, deep in meditation. The guru, an ethereal woman dressed entirely in white, called out to the crowd. "What you look for is here!" The wind began to blow steadily. "Ask for what you seek!"

Bernie took a deep breath. He felt the wind wrap around him as he thought, "Help me find someone to love who can love me back."

Faith and Weight Loss (Ashley)
Every few months, Ashley buys a membership to the little gym in town. After a few weeks, the workouts are abandoned with a great sense of anger and shame. And when she surrendered, Ashley's first inclination was to trudge back to the gym and try exercise again.

Instead, Ashley called her mom and told her how unhappy she was. In the past, these conversations veered between Ashley angrily recounting how her mom had taught her to eat as a child, and Ashley's mom trying to convince her daughter that she was loved, regardless of her size and shape. But this time,

49

Ashley's mother said something completely unexpected, "Honey, why don't we pray?"

Ashley hadn't been to church in years and felt a wave of shame wash over her. "Oh, that's OK, Mom. Don't worry about…"

Her mother's tone of voice surprised Ashley. It was calm but commanding. "Then you just listen, girl. Cause my baby's not gonna live this life hatin' herself. You just listen."

Ashley sat down in her kitchen, a smear of grease still on the wall from where she'd thrown the pizza against it a few days ago. She heard her mother ask God to help her daughter. She listened as her mother told God that her baby was in pain and nothing else had worked.

She was very, very quiet as her mother said, "With all humility, Lord, I ask you to help my baby love herself the way I love her."

The most shocking thing for Ashley was not her mother's prayer but to hear herself whisper, "Amen."

To sum up about faith…

It's worth saying one more time…you don't have to be religious to have spiritual faith. You can believe what you want. Pray to whomever or whatever you like. If you insist on believing that spirituality and religion are the same thing, you are only short changing yourself.

The weird thing is that you don't really even have to believe to get started. Just go through the motions. Say a little prayer. Walk in nature. Just spend a few minutes being quiet and still in the morning. All you have to do is make a little space in your life, stay open-minded, and try. If you've really surrendered to the fact that the problems in your life are making you miserable and desperate, you're in the perfect state to find some answers in God.

At the very worst, you might discover an activity in your life that you enjoy. Meditation or spending some time out in the sunshine…how bad can that be? What would you lose right now if you closed your eyes, took a deep breath and said, "God, please help me."

I had a terrible experience with organized religion and
now you're telling me that the answer is to go back to
that??!!

You're not listening. Nobody is talking about religion
here. I'm talking about a spiritual belief that there is
something in the world that is more capable of running
your life than you are. And, no offense but, given your
track record, it shouldn't be so hard to believe.

Faith Worksheet

My idea of God or a Higher Power is:

_____

_____

_____

_____

_____

Who is a person who loved me unconditionally? What would they want for me?

_____

_____

_____

_____

_____

If God were to help me with this problem, what would happen?

_____

_____

_____

_____

_____

53

Tips on Faith

- Stay open-minded.
- Make your faith personal. This doesn't mean abandoning your particular religious beliefs; instead, think of images (nature, loved ones, etc.) that represent them.
- Embrace activities such as prayer and meditation even if they seem awkward at first.
- Find a regular time in your day to explore faith and spirituality.
- Be patient. After all, how long has your problem troubled you? Your prayers may not be answered in a day. And they may be answered in ways that look very different than what you have in mind.

Mantra

Please help me to _____.

Tool – Prayer

If you have never been religious, you may not know how to pray. In my opinion, it does not matter if you kneel when you pray or say your prayers out loud. Make up your own prayers or use the ones listed at the end of this book – it makes no difference. The most basic prayer is, "Please help me."

If you want to get started, here is a short prayer that you might try. You can read it aloud or say it silently or just read it and stay quiet for a moment.

I don't know who you are.
I don't know who you meant for me to be.
I don't know what path to take.

I am willing to accept that you exist.
I know that you want me to be happy.
I know you can show me a better path.

I choose to let you into my life.
I choose to give you what I've have always kept to myself.
I choose to change.

Please show me the way.

CHAPTER THREE
RESPONSIBILITY

Your problem has been coloring every moment of your day. It has ruined your life, or so it seems. Everything good and hopeful in your life has been shot through with the pain of your problem.

You've been really honest about the fact that you, on your own, cannot resolve the situation. You're open to the idea that perhaps there is some force in the universe that cares for you and is willing to help. And, most importantly, you've asked that force – be it God or a Higher Power or Nature – for help.

Now it's time to stop being a victim and get to work. You thought your God or Higher Power was going to do all the work and gift-wrap a solution for you? Unfortunately, God doesn't do deliveries. We have to do the work and open a space in our lives for change to occur. Much of that work involves taking *responsibility* for our part in creating and perpetuating our own problems. Only when we have learned to take responsibility can we avoid continuing the pattern.

It's no wonder that we have a hard time taking responsibility as adults; from the time we are children, we learn to avoid it. Remember when the teacher turned on the class and asked, "Who did that?" over some minor infraction or silly noise. Nobody wanted to raise their hand. Being responsible isn't fun sometimes.

How would the world be different if people admitted they were human and regularly made mistakes? How many wars, scandals, and lawsuits could be avoided or made less severe? Similarly, many workplace dramas, divorces, and broken families would simply not exist if we all took responsibility for our mistakes.

But we live in a culture of victimhood. It is so appealing to blame our problems on others. But the culture of victimhood comes with the terrible price tag of stifling change and growth. After all, a victim is a helpless creature, simply thrown about by fate and unable to change course.

Our characters are going to give us specific examples of taking responsibility, but let's take a quick look at an area where people are resistant to seeing their part in creating their own problems. Dating and romance is an area where we all have complaints.

Lots of us have lots of dates and hate the process. I know I did before I found the right person to spend my life with. Dating brings up all those fears that hang out around our love lives. And those fears spur on plenty of bad behavior.

Have you ever gone on a dinner date and, before the appetizer arrives, already compiled a long list of judgments about the person across the table, completely sure that the whole thing is a disaster? When I've had one of those grueling evenings, it is easy to make it into a funny story or to moan to my friends about what a jerk the other person was. But the reality is that I chose to be there. And, really, what could I have learned about that other person in so short a time to be so sure it wouldn't work out? Wasn't I being superficial and judgmental based on criteria I would hate to be applied to me?

What about the dates when you feel compelled to tell every last dark and dirty secret while waiting for the movie to start? On those evenings, I inevitably felt slightly sick to my stomach as I watched my date's eyes open wide in horror and then gloss over as I launched

58

into more and more inappropriate information. I knew what I was doing but felt compelled to keep rolling out the stories. Wasn't I driven by my feelings of shame, sure it would all come out eventually so I might as well be rejected right away?

And, of course, we all seem to get very picky when it comes to finding a mate. You've heard the complaints. "Nobody wants to commit. Everybody's flaky. All I want is a nice, stable person to sit at home and watch TV with. IS THAT TOO MUCH TO ASK?" With so many of us out there looking for love, it's hard to believe that there is no one who wants what I want. Maybe I need to take responsibility for the fact that I have a little problem with commitment myself. Maybe I'm looking for a fantasy rather than a real person.

All of this is to say that the Principle of responsibility can work wonders when it comes to changing the behavior that we have some power over – our own. Your problem may be in the area of work or parenting or health, rather than love, but responsibility can help you address those problems just as well.

I don't think any of us truly want to be victims. But most of us are so busy resenting the world for our problems that we never consider our part in creating them, or making them worse. Be prepared to feel resistant to using the principle of responsibility—most people are. This is also the part of the work where you're most likely to get pissed-off and stop. Don't!

You'll need to break out your Feelings List again and use it with the Responsibility Worksheet at the end of this chapter.

Helen

Helen's grudges are like a warm blanket on a cold night. She is deeply comforted by her disdain for men who just want a little sex and no commitment. Self-righteousness shields her from any responsibility. "I'm not asking for prince charming – just a regular schlub who can walk me down the aisle before I need a cane to get there!"

Despite what she says, Helen has never tried dating "a regular schlub." Instead of normal guys, she dates stereotypes – The Jock, The Tycoon, The Biker – in the way a man would date The Model or The Stewardess. (Yes, women can be just as superficial as men.)

In reality, some of these bad boys were actually interested in a relationship. But, for Helen, somehow the thrill was gone as soon as she sensed they were interested. It was the chase that she loved. And, inevitably, once she got to know The Jock or The Tycoon or The Biker, they turned into regular guys with all sorts of flaws and vulnerabilities. Of course, Helen didn't care for that.

If Helen wants to make better choices in men, she needs to take responsibility for her troubled romantic history. Helen laughingly admits to her

61

girlfriends that she is neurotic and spoiled. But does she really want to be with the kind of guy who would want to be with her? Helen is attracting the same type of person she presents to the world – a real piece of work – selfish, superficial, and operating out of fear.

If Helen really took responsibility, she might even question whether she's ready for a relationship. Of course, that would mean facing her childishness and admitting that her mother might be right. It might also mean that she would change.

Helen Takes Responsibility
When she uses the "responsibility worksheet" found at the end of this chapter, Helen stops being a victim and sees the part she has played in creating her problems:

I hate the surfer because he never called me back after we had sex. This makes me feel abandoned, broken-up, cynical and helpless. My responsibility in this is that I was childish – I saw a handsome guy and wanted him. I didn't care whether or not he was "marriage material" and, when he wasn't, it made me ashamed.

I resent my mother because she criticizes my choices in men. This makes me feel ashamed and defensive. My

62

responsibility in this is that I know she's right and that make me furious. And because she still supports me financially, it makes me feel like an immature loser.

I judge men because they just want sex. This makes me feel damaged, dirty, lonely and rejected. My responsibility in this is that sometimes I only want sex too and I think that is wrong. Am I too superficial and lazy to do the work it takes to have a real relationship?

Helen Takes Contrary Action
This week, just to see how it feels, Helen will ask out a guy who might actually want a relationship.

<u>Tom</u>
Tom's anger is like a spray gun, indiscriminately coating everything with rage. Over the years, people have started to avoid him because he just sucks the air out of a room with his selfishness and self-obsession.

If Tom took a deep breath and looked around at work, he would notice that his boss isn't a jerk to everybody at the company. The reality is that Tom just doesn't like bosses. They tell him what to do and he has a hard time with that. In fact, Tom has had the

63

same problems with every boss he's ever had. Tom thinks *he* should be the boss.

Instead of simply doing his job and following directions, Tom gets caught up in an escalating cycle of laziness and arrogance. The angrier he becomes, the more frequently he is late for work and the more unpleasant he becomes when criticized about his failing job performance.

Tom's boss may be a jerk but there is plenty of responsibility to go around. Now that slavery has been abolished, Tom could also look for another job if he's so unhappy in this one. Or he could try being a good employee instead of wallowing in self-pity.

As for his terrible commute, no one forced Tom to buy a house in suburbia when he could have purchased a condo in town. Tom spends a lot of time judging other drivers who are talking on their phones but Tom's road rage seems to disappear when he himself needs to make an important cell phone call while driving.

Tom needs to take a look at why he thinks the world should revolve around him. He needs to take responsibility for his life instead of hiding behind his arrogant rage.

Tom Takes Responsibility

Using the Responsibility Worksheet, Tom is going to find out that he is not such a superior human being that he can sit in judgment on the rest of the human race. What a relief!

I hate my boss because he rages and says I don't do a good job. This makes me feel defensive, guilty, irate and stupid. My responsibility in this is that I don't do a good job because I think this job is below me and that I'm smarter than my boss. I am arrogant.

I can't stand my job because it is so far away from my house. This makes me feel exhausted and pissed-off. My responsibility in this is that I was grandiose and had to have a big house, no matter how long the commute, when I would have probably been happier in a condo near work.

I hate other drivers because they talk on their cell phones while driving. This makes me feel outraged and superior. My responsibility in this is that I do the same thing but I'm so selfish that I only think my own calls are important. I've never thought the rules applied to me because I'm special.

65

Tom Takes Contrary Action

No matter how much he resents his boss, Tom is going to do a good job at work this week and see how he feels on Friday.

<u>Marlene</u>

Whenever she hears the word adoption, Marlene steams with indignation. "People don't know what it means to have your OWN child…your own FLESH and BLOOD." They don't realize the sacrifices she's made so that her family can be perfect.

But is anyone, other than Marlene, all that concerned with life being perfect? If Marlene thinks back, she has always been pretty uncomfortable with the messiness of real life. For example, Marlene loved being a lawyer and was a darned good one. But, once her daughter was born, she couldn't be both a superstar lawyer and a great mom at the same time. And to be less than perfect at either one was unacceptable…so Marlene gave up a job she loved.

Marlene has quite a competitive streak as well. Her sister produced an angelic boy and an adorable girl a few years back, both of whom look like they could be

66

models for Baby Gap. The thought of her own daughter being paired with an adopted son, especially one of another race, makes Marlene burn with jealousy.

And if Marlene wanted to really take responsibility, she would look at the fact that her marriage hasn't been happy for some time now. She and her husband were so honest with each other at the beginning of their marriage but, after a while, they just stopped talking. Of course, the birth of her daughter brought a rush of closeness, but that wore off pretty quickly. Now Marlene just keeps a frozen smile on her face instead of talking to her husband about what's really going on.

Taking responsibility would mean looking at why she really wants to have another child so, if she does, Marlene and her family can be happy.

Marlene Takes Responsibility
To make up for her insecurity, Marlene still pretends she is superwoman. In reality, the only person she's fooling is herself. Time to get real.

I hate myself for not being able to get pregnant again. This makes me feel questioning, shattered, and uneasy.

My responsibility in this is that I don't know why I want this baby. I might want this baby for selfish reasons.

I envy my sister for having two perfect children while I only have one. This makes me feel jealous and unhappy. My responsibility in this is that I've been in a competition with my sister since she was born. I want what she has and I want it for the wrong reasons.

I resent my husband because he works outside the house. This makes me feel thwarted, pessimistic and immature. My responsibility in this is that I chose to stop working because I thought it was the right thing to do, not because it was the right thing for me. I really, really miss working.

Marlene Takes Contrary Action
Marlene is going to call up her sister, be as honest as she can about her feelings, and ask her for advice.

Bernie

So Bernie is in love again. This time it's a 23-year-old closeted trainer from the gym who wants an acting career. This guy's resume makes even Bernie a little nervous…so he's running off to Aspen Gay Ski Week.

You'd think it would be easy for Bernie to take responsibility for his love life. Instead, he is convinced that "gay guys are all crazy and relationship-phobic." If he wants to see the real problem, all Bernie needs to do is step in front of a mirror and repeat that statement.

Poor Bernie is completely responsible for the fact that most nights he goes to sleep not only alone but lonely. In the real world, couples with an age difference of more than twenty years often face challenges. In Hollywood, they face disaster.

Because Bernie still wanders around the world believing he is the "fag" that his grade school classmates called him, he needs to constantly be in control and prove them wrong. It is so much easier to buy love in someone younger than to genuinely find it in someone his own age.

When confronted, Bernie often says, "Hey, I like pretty things! What can I say?" Responsibility for Bernie would mean looking at his superficiality in wanting to be with objects instead of men…and the truth isn't going to be pretty.

The hard truth of the world is that we can't control it, no matter how powerful we might be. Bernie

69

may be able to get the best table in a restaurant or a meeting with a powerful studio exec but he can't make a young hunk love him for the right reasons.

What Bernie can change is himself, and he will start that process by taking responsibility.

Bernie Takes Responsibility

For all of his spiritual activities, Bernie hasn't become very self-aware. He's afraid he'll hate himself if he looks at the life he's created. But taking responsibility isn't about beating up on yourself, it's about telling the simple truth of your life.

I dislike gay men because they're so bad at relationships. This makes me feel kinky, lonely and miserable. My responsibility in this is that I've never once asked out a guy my age and that I'm completely selfish when it comes to sex.

I resent the guys who have rejected me. This makes me feel heartbroken, offended and puzzled. My responsibility in this is that I never really loved those guys and I knew they couldn't love me. I wanted to control them and be in charge.

70

I hate all the kids who called me a pervert in school and beat me up. This makes me feel insecure, ruined and sickened. My responsibility is that I believed them and lived my life accordingly.

Bernie Takes Contrary Action
Bernie is going to ask out an attractive man his own age and see what happens.

<u>Ashley</u>
Let's be very clear about something. Ashley's problem is not that she is overweight. Her problem is that she is unhappy. Ashley's mother, father, and two sisters have gone through plus-sized lives very happily. The superficial judgments strangers might have of her can't compare to the horrible insults Ashley screams silently at herself.

The truth is that Ashley has never completed a single goal in her life and she is deeply ashamed of herself. Losing weight is only one of the many goals she has abandoned. Ashley is smart but she dropped out of college. Ashley likes to read but never finishes a book. Ashley starts to paint her bedroom and stops after doing the trim.

71

For all of her sweetness, Ashley is lazy. Ashley hates admitting that she is lazy because that's what the world thinks of fat people...but she is. This doesn't mean that she is a bad person; it's just that she has allowed one *broken behavior* (we'll be talking a lot more about broken behaviors in the next chapter) to entirely rule her life. Everywhere she looks, she is reminded that a lack of ambition keeps her from her dreams.

For Ashley, taking responsibility for her laziness might mean finally realizing that she does not have to let her feelings define her. She can take contrary action and practice completing goals. And completing goals, however modest they might be, will make it more difficult for Ashley to hate herself.

After all, the skydiver feels fear but jumps anyway. The factory worker is tired but shows up for work. The actress is insecure but still steps onto the stage. Our feelings don't need to hold us back.

Ashley Takes Responsibility
Ashley needs to drop "victim" from her vocabulary and take responsibility:

I resent my mother because she taught me to eat
trashy, fattening food. This makes me feel despairing,

72

robbed and righteous. My responsibility is still acting like a baby! I don't have to eat the same things I ate as a child.

I can't stand men because they judge me based on my outsides. This makes me feel awful, shy and unimportant. My responsibility in this is that I'm just as superficial as they are. I judge myself by my outsides too because inside I know that I've never achieved anything I wanted to.

I hate myself for being a woman. This makes me feel hopeless and weak. My responsibility in this is that I've always felt incomplete without a man. If no man wants me, I think I'm worthless.

I hate myself because I abandon all of my dreams. This makes me feel useless, weepy and embarrassed. My responsibility in this is that I'm lazy and childish. I don't know why but I quit everything when it gets hard.

Ashley Takes Contrary Action
Ashley is going to make a fitness goal for one week and follow through with it no matter how she feels.

73

To sum up about responsibility…

"So it's all my fault??!!"

Well…a big part of it is.

OK, now you're mad. Fair enough, be mad. But please try to keep an open mind. It isn't that you're a bad person. You're just as afraid, selfish, self-obsessed, spoiled, judgmental, superficial, greedy and dishonest as everyone else in the world! You're not alone. These are the broken behaviors that have ruled your life and created all this pain.

The good thing about looking at your responsibility in every bad situation is that you can change yourself. And that's really the only thing you can change. If you're like most people, you'll probably recognize that the unappealing characteristics you've displayed in painful situations are old friends of yours. Haven't the same bad, childish behaviors fueled most of your problems in life?

I congratulate you because you are about to give up being a victim. I pray that you dig deep and take a look at your part in the problems that are so painful to you. If you're completely honest with yourself now, you'll be feeling better soon. Take responsibility.

But in the real world people get hurt through no fault of their own. What responsibility do they have?
Although I've tried to keep it light in this book, you're absolutely right. Really terrible things happen to us.

But having experienced some of those things myself, I had to finally admit to myself that I was letting them define me and destroy my life. I was holding those terrible memories as close as possible every moment and making decisions in the present based on events from many years ago. I finally decided I didn't want to carry that burden anymore. I was only continuing to hurt myself when I'd been hurt enough.

Tips on responsibility

- Be honest. We've all done bad things.
- Stop being a victim.
- Think about how refreshing it would be to stop creating problems.
- How invested are you in making sure your problems are never resolved?
- Change is painful.

Mantra
I will look for my part, my responsibility, in every situation.

75

Responsibility Worksheet:

Look for your responsibility in five painful problems in your life (or five aspects of your main problem). I would encourage you to use the Feelings List to really explore your feelings.

You can also use different words to start each entry. You might have a *grudge* toward somebody or *hate* yourself or *resent* another person. Whatever helps you connect emotionally.

> *Sample*: I hate my boss because he screams at me. This makes me feel angry, ashamed and insecure. My responsibility in this is that I am lazy (I could work harder sometimes) and self-obsessed (I've never taken the time to think about why he's so unhappy).

> I would encourage you to copy the Responsibility Worksheet as you might find that, once you get started, you can come up with a lot more than a few examples!

76

I resent _____ because he/she/they
_____. This makes me feel
_____.

My responsibility in this is _____
_____.

I resent _____ because he/she/they
_____. This makes me feel
_____.

My responsibility in this is _____
_____.

I resent _____ because he/she/they
_____. This makes me feel
_____.

My responsibility in this is _____
_____.

I resent _____ because he/she/they
_____. This makes me feel
_____.

My responsibility in this is _____
_____.

Tool - Contrary Action

Most of us let our feelings determine our actions and these actions usually have a negative effect. When I feel threatened and attacked by co-workers, I lash out at them. When I feel fat, I eat even more. When I feel invisible in a room, I isolate myself further. Why do we give our feelings such power over our lives?

The feelings you examined when surrendering to your problem have ruled you for far too long. Just because you have a feeling does not mean that you have to act on it or let it hold you back. Try taking contrary action instead.

Many people we admire use contrary action all the time. The soldier feels fear but still walks onto the battlefield. The performer feels insecure but still takes to the stage. The athlete feels exhausted yet still continues to play. The minister or rabbi feels flawed and human but still carries a message of hope.

Contrary action is simply doing the opposite of what you want to do in a difficult situation. If you feel intimidated by a person, talk to them. If you feel too lazy to go to the gym, go anyway. If your co-worker makes you angry, be kind to them instead of vindictive. Take contrary action and watch your feelings change.

Remember...*feelings are not facts.*

78

CHAPTER FOUR
HONESTY

You thought it was bad you had to own your part in screwing up your life? Now you have to tell another person about it! This is one reason why I encourage you to use *The Principles* with a group of friends. However, you can also talk to a priest or even call up a chat line and spew. But you've got to get this stuff out because it's making you ashamed and you probably think you're the only person who's ever been so petty, nasty, and childish.

You're in for a surprise though. Most human beings mess things up. When we hear another person honestly acknowledge their part in creating their own problems, it is enormously refreshing. Rather than saying "You're a disaster," your friend, clergyman, or the girl on the 976 line is more likely to say, "Me too." Welcome to the human race. You're not alone anymore with your secrets.

79

Honesty is the antidote to one of the most poisonous of feelings – shame. Shame warps us in ways large and small by separating us from other people, creating the false impression that our problems are bigger or worse than those other people have. But, in reality, most human problems are pretty similar and remarkably mundane. You will be amazed by how much simpler it is to be honest and tell another person what's really going on with you.

This process is not something that I've made up. Having the humility to impart shameful information to another person is a ritual at the heart of religions and spiritual practices. In the seventh century, confession became a part of the Catholic Church. The practice allowed penitents to be forgiven privately without performing public penance. At the time, many in the church believed that true confession was meant to be only between the individual and God. However, it clearly fulfilled a powerful need for believers to connect with another human being around their wrongdoings, even if their ultimate petition was to God.

More recently, 12-step programs have made the sharing of bad behavior with another addict a cornerstone of their work. In the 12 steps, the 4th step

80

is a listing of harms done to others under the influence. This list is then read to a trusted friend, sponsor, or spiritual advisor in the 5th step. As the addict enters sober life, he or she often makes more mistakes. These are addressed in the 10th step where the addict continues to "take personal inventory."

Let me share with you my experience with the Principle of honesty. As part of this process, I had written down a long list of people who I resented, hated, and bore grudges against. I was so invested in hating some of these people that I even kept a list of them at one time, telling myself that one day I would get revenge upon them! So it was challenging when I looked at how I myself had created many of the problems I had blamed upon my "enemies."

When I was honest with a friend and read him my list of resentments, he started laughing! Far from being offended, I was relieved because I knew he was laughing out of identification. To my amazement, some of the things he laughed hardest at were my bad behaviors that I had never revealed to another human being. He had done the same things.

I know that you might find it hard to trust another person with this deeply personal information and I do

81

encourage you to pick someone you can trust (or do it completely anonymously on-line). But my experience is that people respond very well to honesty. Most people feel honored when entrusted with this kind of information. So I hope that you will be open to this experience. It has been one of the most rewarding of my life.

Helen Gets Honest About Dating

Helen is blessed with a large group of girlfriends who share her dating woes, and they've all heard a lot of sob stories. Last Sunday, Helen invited them over, ordered in Chinese, and told them she had some stuff to get off her chest.

Helen found that she needed to make some additional copies of her Responsibility Worksheet because she had a lot more than five examples of how she was responsible for her mess of a love life. She explained that she had been using *The Principles* to look at what responsibility she had in creating her tragic love life. Instead of her usual plea for help or sympathy, Helen said, "I just don't want to keep this to myself. So settle in girls, it's gonna be a bumpy ride."

For the next 30 minutes, Helen dumped all of the bad behavior that she had shown in the dating department. It turns out that Helen had blown-off a number of men who were exactly the type she said she was always looking to meet – sincere, hard working, funny, and honest. It was Helen who had been more than a little superficial and dishonest when, over and over again, she had rejected any guy who wasn't Superman with a Porsche.

The only time Helen cried that night was when she admitted that she didn't really know if she wanted a relationship. She liked that her house was a showplace with no dirty socks lying around. She wasn't interested in watching football games. And, when it came right down to it, she kind of liked her freedom.

Helen's friends didn't quite know what to make of this display. One was deeply threatened and pretended to have a migraine. Another asked to borrow Helen's copy of *The Principles*.

Tom Gets Honest About Work

Not being one for encounter groups or weepy talks with his buddies, Tom took his Responsibility Worksheet to his priest. Having heard his share of confessions, the priest was not in the least shocked when Tom said he needed to get honest with at least one other person about what was going on. The priest simply nodded and settled back into his chair.

Tom told the priest about the level of rage he had toward his boss. But, more importantly, Tom talked about his rage toward himself. Somehow, Tom had held onto the childish idea that the world was going to wake up one day and realize that King Tom was in

84

charge. Since Tom had been a boy, he'd been a little bully. "My way or the highway," had always been Tom's motto.

Tom also got a double-whammy in the broken behavior department because he was both lazy and arrogant. He had just assumed that his company would promote him to an executive level because of his natural talent, never realizing that success was more about hard work and commitment than being a genius. Tom's dirty little secret was that, when good things happened for other people, even people he liked, Tom felt nothing but jealousy and anger. "Why not me?" was the question that rang in his head every day.

Tom also got honest with the priest about how painful life had become, about how he felt like a psycho driving to the grocery store, and that he finally wanted to change and feel some relief.

The priest smiled and nodded.

Marlene Gets Honest About Parenting
Marlene dropped her daughter at her sister's house for a day because she wanted to spend some time alone with her husband. It was cold and rainy so they built a fire and had a lazy day reading. As it was getting dark,

85

Marlene told her husband that she needed to talk. He looked a little panicked but Marlene said, "Don't worry. This is totally about me. I just need to be honest with you."

Marlene didn't read off of her Responsibility Worksheet although she had filled it out dutifully and precisely, as only a lawyer would. She was afraid that it would freak out her husband and she wanted to tell him everything as simply as she could.

Marlene stressed again that none of what she was going to say was about blaming her husband. Instead, she wanted to take responsibility for a lot of lies she had been telling herself.

Maybe the most important thing Marlene said that day was that she was deeply jealous of her husband's career and really missed working. She said that she felt ashamed, like it made her a bad mother, but that she desperately wanted to work again and wasn't sure whether she wanted to have another baby.

That big admission was weirdly easy for Marlene. Much more difficult was admitting to her husband that a lot of her life had been about being in a petty competition with her sister. It seemed so childish when she heard herself admitting these things, but Marlene also recognized that they were completely true.

86

The only thing Marlene's husband had to say was, "I know. And I love you."

Bernie Gets Honest About Dating

Bernie felt sick after he filled out his Responsibility Worksheet. He felt like the worst person on the face of the world. He felt hopeless and ashamed. And there was no way he was ever going to share this with another person. Instead, Bernie decided to spend a little time trawling the Internet chat rooms to see if he could find a little "afternoon delight." Bernie had always lied about his age on-line, advertising himself as "late-30s, gym bod" when the reality was "early 50s, cute, with a gut." (He convinced himself that everyone lied on-line and everyone understood you had to add at least a decade onto the listed age.) And he was very clear in his profile that he was only interested in "under 30."

A few weeks ago, "MatureMacho" began to send Bernie messages on-line. Bernie ignored him as soon as he saw that the guy's profile listed him as being "mid-50s." That alone sent a shiver up Bernie's spine.

Today, however, when a message from MatureMacho popped-up ("Howz it goin?"), Bernie

87

responded with "U really wanna know?" For the next hour, Bernie tapped away on his keyboard and told MatureMacho every nasty secret that had been written down on the Responsibility Worksheets.

Every few minutes, Bernie typed in, "This too heavy?"

But MatureMacho was a good cyber listener and the response was always, "Nope. Keep goin, man."

Bernie had finally told another person, another gay man, what he really thought about other gay people and about himself.   Then he added MatureMacho to his permanent Buddy List.

Ashley Gets Honest About Her Weight
Ashley is selectively honest. Her best girlfriend, who is stick thin, gets the eating sob stories. Her younger sister, who is about as deep as thin crust pizza, is awarded the *men are so superficial* conversation. In other words, Ashley makes sure she discusses her problems with people who have absolutely no idea what she is talking about and, therefore, aren't likely to dig too deeply.

After she finished her Responsibility Worksheet, she could only think of one person she would be willing

88

to share it with. Ashley's Aunt Laura had spent her life fighting the battle of the bulge, had been scandalously married three times, and was actively on the look-out for number four. As black sheep of the family, Aunt Laura was voted the person most likely to understand but least likely to judge.

When Ashley stopped by Aunt Laura's house on a Saturday afternoon, Laura thought it was for cake, coffee, and family gossip. Instead, Ashley hauled out her Responsibility Worksheet and said, "Girl, just stay calm 'cause this isn't gonna be pretty."

And indeed it wasn't. Ashley talked about how she had spent her life blaming her weight problems on mom's sinfully delicious mac 'n cheese when, in reality, Ashley had been eating her way through all her feelings of laziness and disappointment.

She told Laura about how she thought men were shallow pigs but, just as Laura started nodding, Ashley launched into exactly what she thought of herself, "I haven't finished one thing I've started in life and I pretty much hate myself. So how is someone else gonna love me?"

Aunt Laura cried that day. And then they had cake.

To sum up about honesty…

We all hear a lot about honesty and nothing is more insulting than to be called a liar. But, guess what? Most of us lie pretty consistently and for no good reason. It's actually out of habit. Our lies can be outright: "I've never cheated on you!" They can take the form of secrets: "I sit at my desk looking at porn most of the day when I'm supposed to be working." Or they can be lies of omission: that's when you only tell part of the truth, usually the part that is comfortable. But, let's face it, they're all just lies.

Here's the good news. If you are willing to read the work you did on your Responsibility Worksheet to another person, even if it is a completely anonymous person on-line, you've already taken a step toward honesty. And, as you clean up some of the chaos in your life during the rest of *The Principles* process, it will become easier and easier to be honest…both with yourself and others.

I've found that, ultimately, it's simpler to be honest. Who has time to keep track of which stories I've told to which people? And, generally, people respond to honesty. It's amazing that we don't practice this Principle more consistently in everyday life.

Wait a minute! In the real world, we need to defend ourselves. If I'm honest and vulnerable with somebody, they can use it against me!

Then make better choices about who you're honest with, my friend. If you can't find one person in the whole world to be completely honest with, you're in deep trouble. And if that person is a stranger you talk to on-line, so be it. At least you won't be alone, dragging around those secrets anymore.

Tips on Honesty

- Being honest doesn't need to involve hurting people. You can always find someone to talk to who won't be hurt by the truth you need to share.
- Don't apologize for your honesty.
- Don't attack or be a victim. What you are talking about has to do with you and the responsibility that you're taking for your problems.
- Pick someone to talk with whom you can trust to keep your confidence.
- Remember that secrets, shame and lies will only lead to worse problems.

Mantra

Today I will find one person to be honest with about
_____.

Honesty Worksheet

These are the people I can be honest with about my responsibility for creating my own problems:

_____

_____

_____

If I can't be honest with someone I know, here are the places I can be honest anonymously:

_____

_____

_____

What is my worst fear about being honest?

_____

_____

_____

What is the deepest secret that I have that I have told myself no one would ever find out and that no one would ever be able to understand?

_____

_____

_____

Tool – Letting Go of Self-Obsession

So much of our fear about being honest is about self-obsession. What will he think of me? Will they tell someone else? The reality is that most people could care less about the petty little secrets and lies that we have been guarding so closely for all these years.

In fact, we are being selfish when we keep our problems to ourselves and pretend to be perfect people who have it all together. How will our friends, co-workers, and loved ones ever feel free to be honest about what they are going through if we don't do it ourselves?

In my experience, what happens when I am honest is that barriers come down between me and other people. It is not selfish at all to talk about my problems if I am willing to be honest. Because honesty opens a dialogue. Honesty is not moaning and groaning about the same tired old problem for years! What a relief for my loved ones to hear that I can see that I'm part of the problem and that I want to change.

In the modern world, we are understandably concerned with protecting ourselves, and part of that impulse is to be secretive. But I believe honesty is a

94

much stronger position. If I am an open book, with nothing to hide, it is very difficult for anyone else to harm me. Honesty creates real strength rather than bravado.

CHAPTER FIVE
HUMILITY

So you've taken responsibility, been honest, and aired your dirty laundry. But you're still faced with a nagging question – *why'd I do it?* Nearly everyone, with the exception of certain saints, has a few persistent and highly unattractive habits that continually nudge them toward making bad choices. People call these habits sins or character defects. I like to think of them as *broken behaviors* – the stuff that clearly messes me up but I keep doing anyway.

So what does a broken behavior look like in reality? We'll check back with our five characters as they practice humility in identifying and letting go of their broken behaviors, but here are some quick examples. Maybe you're still letting your parents support you at age 30 but resenting the heck out of them. You're *lazy* and *childish*. Wonder why you think it's OK to honk your horn like a crazy person except when you're the one who goes into a "cell phone coma" behind the wheel? You're *arrogant*. Pushing 50 but still dating 20-year-olds and wondering why it doesn't work out? You're *afraid* and *superficial*.

You're not a horrible person. You're using broken behaviors. Now, for the first time in your life, you're reflecting on them and seeing their nasty effects.

Although I am not Jewish, I find the Jewish view of sinfulness very useful. Unlike Catholicism, Judaism does not believe we are born with some kind of original sin but, rather, that our natural human instincts can run amok and become sinful. In Jewish teachings, sin is called *het* and translates as "something that has gone astray." This is a fairly good way to look at broken behaviors. It does not imply that I am inherently sinful but rather suggests that, if my human instincts are not reigned in, they can become destructive and take me away from a spiritual life.

Whether you call this kind of behavior sin or character defect or broken behavior, it's one thing to see it and quite another to say you are so totally sick of yourself that you want to change. If you have the humility to see yourself as you really are, you might ask your Higher Power to help you change.

Humility is a difficult Principle for most people to grasp. Many mistake it for humiliation while others think

97

it means taking a vow of poverty in a monastery! But, for me, humility can be expressed in the phrase, "Get over yourself." When I see how tiresome and destructive my bad habits have become, I am literally "over myself." And if I admit that, like all people, I have instincts that have gotten out of control, I can stop thinking that I am so unique. For me, humility comes with seeing that, like everybody else, I have great parts to my personality and some that should really be discarded. I'm no better and no worse that my fellow man.

So dig deep into your broken behaviors and you will probably find enough humility to ask for help. Actually, you've already done part of this work – your broken behaviors are listed in each entry on your Responsibility Worksheet. They are what you took responsibility for. Check out the Tool Kit list of broken behaviors for help in identifying more of them and then use the Humility Worksheet to start changing them.

Helen, Humility, and Dating

Helen shoved those Responsibility Worksheets as far back in a dresser drawer as they would go. But she kept thinking about them. The most disturbing thing on them was not all the bad choices she'd made about men; it was that she'd seen a pattern. She had always thought of her life as a big madcap adventure when it turns out that it had been a fairly pedestrian cycle of the same broken behaviors – again and again and again.

The broken behavior that Helen liked the least was that she was *childish*. A strong, sexy, educated woman childish? Yep. Helen kept running back to mommy in New York for funds she ended up spending on cocktails and Manolo Blahniks. Helen thought of all the "daddy types" she'd dated and wondered if she picked them because she'd never made her own way in the world.

Then there was *superficial*. That was a killer because Helen had always loved attacking men for that very same broken behavior. "They can't see past my breasts!" It turns out that Helen has a pretty hard time seeing past biceps and Porsches.

Helen had it in her head that being ashamed of her behavior was a good thing. But she realized that her shame actually let her beat up on herself rather than

99

change. Helen wanted to replace her bad behaviors with something to be proud of. So she sat down with her favorite photo of her dad, who'd passed away, and thought about what kind of daughter he would have been proud of.

"Dad, please help me to stop being childish and superficial and ashamed. Help me to be mature and thoughtful - a daughter you would be proud of."

Tom, Humility, and Work

Tom felt fantastic for almost a week after he told his priest about the mess he'd been making of his life. He felt like he wasn't alone. He'd been peaceful. Then his boss asked him to work late one night, with no advance notice, and Tom had a meltdown and got fired.

Since then Tom's had quite a bit of free time to examine his Responsibility Worksheets and reflect on his decisions. As he no longer has to drive to work, he can't blame his frustrations on traffic anymore. Tom is just left with himself and his broken behaviors.

Somehow Tom got it into his head when he was a kid that he was just a little bit better than the rest of the world. If he wasn't the captain of the team, he didn't want to play. If he wasn't dating the most popular girl,

100

he preferred to stay at home. Life was a big competition for Tom and, in his eagerness to win, he'd become an *arrogant* jerk.

Of course, it's pretty hard to be arrogant without being *grandiose* and *superior* too. For example, Tom would be horrified to live in some rental close to work instead of residing in the prestigious suburb where his house is shaded by lush trees. Did the drive torture him? Yes. Could he afford it? Just barely. But none of that mattered because Tom had to make sure the world knew he was on top.

When it came right down to it, Tom's ex-wife had hit the nail on the head when she told him that she didn't want to be with someone who was so fundamentally *selfish*. Well, now that Tom has paid such a high price to hang onto his broken behaviors, he is a little more willing to change. Sometimes we have to get beaten into humility.

Marlene, Humility, and Parenting
Marlene had always taken great pride in her selflessness. As a daughter, she had always taken care of her parents. As a mother, she had given up her work to care for her daughter. As a wife, she was the

101

one who sacrificed her career to make a beautiful home for her husband.

The problem was that Marlene was, by nature, actually a *selfish* person. She resented always having to think of other people and to prioritize their needs. So why did she do it?

Somewhere along the way, Marlene had decided that life was a competition for the World's Most Perfect Person. She had to be the best wife, the best mother, and the best daughter – as if someone were keeping score. Marlene doesn't know why but she always had *low self-esteem*: striving for perfection seemed to help balance out how she really felt inside.

Marlene's competitive streak really came out when she was around her sister. Marlene's sister was distracted, a little sloppy, and very happy. If her house was a mess, Marlene's sister just laughed when guests stopped by. If her daughter was throwing a tantrum, Marlene's sister intuitively knew the right way to be both kind and stern. It seemed as if her sister didn't really care what the world thought and, with that attitude, lived with a kind of grace.

Late at night, with both her daughter and husband deep asleep, Marlene sat in the moonlight in her living room and prayed. In the quiet of her home,

102

Marlene looked at her Responsibility Worksheets and prayed, "Please help me to be the person I know I can be."

Bernie, Humility, and Dating
Bernie has a bad habit of having long conversations with himself in his head. Since he read (well, typed) his Responsibility Worksheets to his on-line friend MatureMacho, he has been debating with himself.

"You're *superficial*. All you care about is pretty people, pretty things..."

"Yeah, what's your point?"

"Well, if every guy you meet is an object, can you care about them?"

"Am I supposed to?"

"Don't be glib with me, missy. I know how you feel."

"Well, maybe I am a little *lonely*."

"There ya go, girl."

"Oh, why bother. Just the way it is. Nobody wants me."

"Oh, boo-hoo-hoo. Skip the pity party."

"It's my *self-pity* party and I'll cry if I want to."

"If only you would. Just let it all out."

"Sometimes I think if I really cry, I'll never stop. I just hate myself."

"Oh, honey, *self-hatred's* a young man's game. It just takes too much energy to try and destroy your life."

"I'm so sick of myself. Why don't I just change?"

"Want to?"

"I sure as hell do."

"Me too."

Ashley, Humility, and Weight

Ashley's house is pink, pink, *pink*! Her bed is accessorized with pink ruffles and pink fluffy pillows. Her kitchen has a pink teapot and rose-colored dishes. Her bathroom has wallpaper covered in pink flamingos. Ashley woke up this morning, opened her eyes, and gasped, "My God, who lives here? A 12-year-old?"

Ashley got dressed. Her closet was awash in lacy blouses, pastel sweaters, flower print dresses and Mary Janes. Looking at herself in the mirror, she thought, "I look like a plus-sized Laura Ashley ad."

"When did I get so girly?" Ashley wondered. Thinking back, she was actually something of a tomboy as a kid. But the fatter she got, the more feminine and

104

soft she became. Being *childish* and hyper-girly, she decided, had become her way to deal with being overweight.

The word childish brought with it a flood of other broken behaviors. Children don't have to be deep and serious – nobody would ever accuse a kid of being *superficial*. People don't expect kids to finish things – children are almost expected to be a little *lazy* and easily distracted.

Since the first time she used the Feelings List and picked out the word *feminine*, Ashley knew something was up with her weight and her identity as a woman. Sitting in her pink clothes in her pink house, Ashley decided that she wanted to be a woman, not a little girl. Ashley thought of how her mother had prayed to God for her daughter to love herself. Ashley repeated that prayer in her head and added, "Help me be a woman I can respect, not a little girl."

To sum up about humility…

If you're like most people, you hear the word *humility* and think *humiliation*. And it can certainly be humiliating to become aware of all the petty, childish behavior that has been creating our problems. But once we've surrendered to how bad those problems have become, taken responsibility for our part in them, and shared them honestly with another person, we are ready to transform humiliation back into humility.

Remember that you're not in this alone. You've gotten sick enough of your broken behaviors that you are going to ask your God or Higher Power or nature or…whatever is out there…to help you change. If you've been really honest during this process, you should be pretty willing to change by now.

The Humility Worksheet along with the list of broken behaviors (in the Tool Kit section immediately after the Feelings List) will help you identify the particular behaviors that are driving your problems. They should be pretty clearly listed in the work you did on the Responsibility Worksheet as well. The rest is up to you and your Higher Power.

Oh great, so I'm supposed to just wake up and change in one day? I've been acting this way my whole life!

And aren't you sick of it? You probably don't believe it but it actually is possible to change immediately. Let's go back to the idea of contrary action described earlier. If you are childish, make mature decisions today. If you are jealous, congratulate people on their accomplishments. Practice. After a while, your feelings will change to match your new behavior.

Tips on Humility

- Practice acting like someone who doesn't have the broken behavior that drives your problem.
- Expect your broken behavior to come back. Then start over again.
- Stay out of self-pity and self-righteousness. You're no better or worse than anybody else. You're human.
- Remember that there is a difference between humility and humiliation.
- Allow yourself to want a better life than your old behavior has given you.

Mantra

Please help me to change the habits that mess up my life. I am willing to change.

Humility Worksheet

What are the top three broken behaviors that have created your problem?

(Use the list from your Tool Kit.)

_____

_____

_____

What are the opposite behaviors to these broken behaviors?

(Example: Dishonesty/Honesty)

_____

_____

_____

What are three actions you could take to practice these new behaviors?

_____

_____

_____

What would your life look like if you no longer had the broken behaviors that have created your problem?

_____

_____

_____

Tool – Stop Being a Victim

So much of using *The Principles* involves removing the word victim from your vocabulary. The problem with being a victim is you're screwed! If the world is out to get you, if everyone hates you, if nobody understands you...well, there's not much hope, is there?

On the other hand, if you're not a victim but, instead, are willing to accept that you and your bad behaviors have created your own problems, then there is great hope. Because *you* can change *you*. In fact, you are the only thing in the world that you have any control over.

You started to change as soon as you saw your responsibility in creating the problem that has tortured you for so long. Identifying your broken behaviors takes that work deeper and let's you see the extent to which things like selfishness and fear have damaged what started out as a pretty good life.

Expect yourself to be resistant to this process and to return sometimes to a victim mentality. There is something comfortable about wallowing in the idea that the world is out to get you; it keeps you frozen with no need to change, and sometimes we enjoy that sick

110

feeling. So don't feel bad when you go back to being a victim; just don't stay there for too long.

The other thing about victims is that they're usually alone and afraid. We don't want you to be in that space anymore. And, indeed, you're not. You have hope for a better life.

CHAPTER SIX
FORGIVENESS

Remember your Responsibility Worksheet? Remember all those people you thought had screwed you over? Remember finding out that you actually played a big part in creating each and every instance? It's not very likely that you're going to lead a happier life with all those messes weighing on your conscience.

The next part of this journey involves cleaning it all up. This is where we begin to see if you really want to change your life because this process, although it may seem difficult, leads to the most rewarding of the Principles – forgiveness. You will forgive others, allowing them to forgive you, and, ultimately, forgive yourself.

Different spiritual and religious organizations utilize this process with great success. 12-step programs call it *making amends*. Churches refer to it as

112

atoning for your sins or paying penance. As the Book of Leviticus states, "You will not exact vengeance on, or bear any sort of grudge against, the members of your race, but will love your neighbor as yourself."

Buddhists, who believe in reincarnation, find forgiveness essential. Ajahn Pasanno of the Abhayagiri Buddhist Monastery says, "If we haven't forgiven, we keep creating an identity around our pain, and that is what is reborn. That is what suffers." In Islam, Allah is the "most forgiving." In Judaism, if a person who has wronged you sincerely apologizes, you are obliged to practice forgiveness.

Hindu texts have a particularly beautiful explanation of the power of forgiveness. Vidura said, "What is there that forgiveness cannot achieve? What can a wicked person do unto him who carries the sabre of forgiveness in his hand? Fire falling on the grassless ground is extinguished of itself."

Reviewing your Responsibility Worksheets, note the people you have grudges toward, including yourself. (I would even include people who have passed away.) It's time for you to make amends to all of these people you've resented for far too long. If you think about it, most of those people are not even aware you're holding

113

a grudge against them. You're the one who spends hours stewing over them, while they happily carry on with their lives. Don't you want to stop wasting all that time and energy?

Most of us have people in our lives who we've resented for years. If you swallow your pride, take responsibility for your part in the problem, and find a way to make amends to them, you will be absolutely astounded at the relief you will feel in every area of your life…including the problem that lead you to this process.

Amends take many forms. With most people it will be in the form of an apology and a pledge not to let it happen again. In other cases, it might involve just treating them better. With people who have died (grudges against parents who have passed away are common, for example), you can write them a letter or visit their grave to make an apology.

You'll probably be amazed at the response, both from the other person and within yourself. A simple "I'm sorry" has the ability to change the world. People are blown-away by someone taking responsibility for their actions. You also might find that the person or situation you've so hated transforms into the best part of your life.

114

What's the magic here? It's called forgiveness and it is one of the most beautiful emotions known to mankind. Everything is possible when we forgive other people and allow them to forgive us. You might even begin to forgive yourself and stop making your life so painful.

Helen Forgives

Helen had been nursing a particularly nasty grudge against the surfer she dated once and never heard from again. "This is ridiculous," she thought, "I barely even got to know him!" Still her resentment toward him was like a bottle of poison she took a little sip from every day; it wasn't enough to kill her but it made her feel sick.

The surfer appeared on Helen's Responsibility Worksheet. The truth was she didn't even really like the guy. He was boring. But he had great abs. Once again, Helen had been as shallow and superficial as all the guys she had judged for treating her the same way.

Helen swallowed her pride and decided she would try to forgive the jerk. She dialed his number, got his voicemail (as usual!), and just said, "Hey, its Helen. I want to talk to you about something. Could you give me a call?"

Naturally, he didn't call back. Helen tried twice more. No luck. Finally, she left a longer message. "Hey, it's me…Helen…your voicemail stalker. Listen, I'm not going to bother you again so let me just leave a message about…OK, here's the thing. I'm calling to say I'm sorry. I never really got to know you when we went out. The truth is I just thought you were this hot

116

surfer guy and that's about all I wanted to know. So, anyway, I'd be turned-off if that's how a guy thought about me so...sorry. And if we ever run into each other again, I hope to get to know you."

The surfer called back in ten minutes. His name's Ed, by the way. Turns out he's a pretty nice guy.

Tom Forgives

If you knew the thoughts that had been going on in Tom's head about his former boss, who canned him, you would probably call the police. Talk about revenge fantasies! Even Tom had to admit that they were keeping him from even looking for a new job because he was so resentful about losing the last one.

Tom called his ex-boss and asked to see him. The guy told Tom in no uncertain terms that there was zero interest in having Tom back at the company. Tom heard himself saying, "I know. And I just want five minutes of your time."

The next afternoon, Tom waited nervously in the conference room, his palms dripping sweat. His boss strode in, still barking instructions to an assistant over his shoulder, slammed the door, sat down and looked at his watch. "You got five minutes, Tom."

Tom swallowed hard and launched into what he knew he had to say, "I'm just...I'm not here to ask for my job back. I wanted to tell you face-to-face that I was an arrogant prick here. I wanted to be the boss, not an employee. I got my paycheck every week but I didn't do a good job and I'm sorry. If there's anything I can do to make up for it, let me know."

Tom had never seen his boss at a loss for words but the guy turned bright red and was looking down. Tom's boss finally asked, "Why'd you want to come here and...say this?"

Tom felt as if he were listening to another person as he heard himself say, "I don't wanna be a jerk anymore. I'm sick of living this way."

Marlene Forgives

Marlene had always been Little Miss Perfect so she didn't have a lot of people to make amends to. She'd been a good mom and a great employee so those areas were clean.

When Marlene told her husband that she was sorry for being such a neurotic mess since having a

118

baby, he told her that the only thing he wanted was for her to do whatever she needed to be happy...because he loved her.

When Marlene told her sister that she was sorry for always being competitive, her sister looked puzzled and said, "Mar, you don't have to compete with me. I think you're amazing. I totally respect you."

Marlene was left with the strange fact that the only person she needed to forgive and be forgiven by was...Marlene. While her daughter was napping, she sat down at the kitchen table and wrote herself a note:

I'm so sorry for being so hard on you. I expected you to be some kind of superwoman. You were supposed to be able to be a mom and a lawyer and a wife and do it all perfectly. That was way too much pressure for anybody. What can I do to make it up to you?

And although she felt *totally* lame, she answered herself:

You can just let me be. Let me have one kid if that's all I can handle. Let me adopt a kid if I can't get pregnant. Let me work part time as a lawyer without all the guilt. Let me be human once in a while.

Marlene agreed to forgive Marlene...

119

Bernie Forgives

Bernie is like a man possessed. He has been running into waiters, out-of-work actors, and aspiring models all over town and apologizing for using them and then throwing them away. Too bad he didn't think his amends through a little more thoroughly because now he has a private chef, owes two actors recurring roles on his new TV show, and had to promise a model an introduction to Karl Lagerfeld. And they all think they have to sleep with Bernie again to collect on the promises. What a mess.

Had Bernie thought through his amends, he might have started from a different place. Because he doesn't resent all those guys that much. He resents the kids who punched and tortured him as a kid. He resents the hell out of his parents who never came to his rescue and his father who, before his death, told Bernie, "I don't care how much money you got, you're still a queer."

Until yesterday, Bernie had never visited his father's grave, after having paid for the most expensive casket, service, and marble headstone he could find. Instead, he walked through each day hating his father and hating himself.

120

Bernie finally went to the cemetery yesterday. Under a perfect blue sky, he sat by his father's grave and made amends to the man he'd thought he would hate forever. Bernie apologized for never showing his father that a gay man could have a loving relationship. More importantly, Bernie told his father that he knew the difference between an apology and an amends. Bernie pledged to *amend* his behavior and lead a life as a gay man that both he and his father could be proud of.

Ashley Forgives

Growing up, Ashley's home life centered around the kitchen. The family was always hanging out, talking, cooking, and especially eating at the weathered old table in the kitchen. Ashley had spent her adult life condemning those warm and happy times as the reason she became overweight.

After Ashley wrote out her Responsibility Worksheets and read them to her aunt, she began to miss her mother. It had been months since Ashley had shown up for the big Sunday dinner her mom cooked every week for the extended family.

So the next Sunday, Ashley surprised her mom by showing up in the early afternoon to help cook. The

121

house was usually a hive of activity but, on that Sunday, it was quiet and Ashley found herself alone in the kitchen with mom.

Mom seemed to spend her whole life at the stove, stirring some huge pot of deliciousness. As mom stirred away, Ashley put her arms around her and whispered in her ear.

"Now don't look at me or I'm gonna get weepy. I gotta tell you something."

Mom just kept stirring so Ashley took a deep breath and went on, "You know I wasted a lot of time blaming you and the family for me being fat. And I wanted to say…I'm sorry Mom. It was real *childish*. I gotta grow up and learn how to not *hate myself*. I wanna stop being so *lazy* and get to work on all the stuff I've been putting off so long. And I want to thank you for your prayers."

Mom just kept on stirring as Ashley kissed away the tears running down her cheeks.

To sum up about forgiveness…

I know I've gone all soft and sugary talking about forgiveness but it's hard not to! When we take responsibility for our problems, give up being victims, get honest with another person and clean up our messes, everything changes. Life opens up.

It's natural to be nervous about talking so honestly to people about how we've messed up and been wrong. That's why we wait until we've done our homework and prepared ourselves. At this point in the process, you should know that just because you are afraid of something doesn't mean you can't do it.

And remember, you're not doing this alone. Hopefully you've found a friend or at least a supportive stranger who you've already shared some deep, dark secrets with. That person is rooting for you to complete this process. More importantly, you have faith that something in the universe – God, a Higher Power, nature, angels – watches over you and wants you to be happy. As you go about cleaning up the messes that you've created, you're not alone.

But what if people are mean to me when I go to make amends to them?

It truly doesn't matter. In the end, this is for you. You are going to own your truth and see if you can make it up to them. If you're sincere in that desire, most people react in a positive way and, if they don't, you still have the satisfaction of knowing you did everything you could. And I have to tell you that, in my experience, every person I made amends to was gracious, loving, and grateful.

Tips on Forgiveness

- Never justify your actions and end up attacking the person you are apologizing to. This is about you and what you've done.
- Be careful to not hurt the other person by telling them something that would cause them pain.
- Pray before you go to make amends.
- Rehearse what you are going to say to make sure that you can be clear and direct.

- Remember that this process is intended to help you lay down those tired old grudges you've been dragging around for years.
- Don't forget to include yourself on the list of people you've harmed. If you take this seriously and do your best, you've begun to forgive yourself for all the pain you've created in your own life.

Mantra

Please help me to start a new life with a clean conscience. Guide me and help me to not be afraid.

Forgiveness Worksheet

These are the people who I have harmed with my broken behaviors:

_____

_____

_____

_____

_____

_____

These are the things I need to say to the people I've harmed:

_____

_____

_____

_____

_____

_____

These are my fears about this part of *The Principles*:

_____

_____

_____

_____

126

Tool – More on forgiveness and amends

12-step programs have particularly good advice for us in the area of forgiveness. Members of these programs are instructed never to make an amends that will harm another person. That would be selfish. For example, if I were having an affair with your wife and you didn't know about it, should I march up to you, tell you what is going on, and apologize? Of course not! That action would harm you, your wife, and your family. Everyone would be better off if I simply ended the affair and was quietly kind to you and your family.

     When I ask forgiveness from another person, I never talk about the things that I feel they have also done to wrong me. This is only about my behavior and me. Many times the other person will also respond with some things they want to take responsibility for, but not always.

     Once you have gone through this process, you will understand that the reaction of the other person is entirely beside the point. You're going to feel a little lighter, a little cleaner, and oddly empowered. After all, you won't have anything to hide anymore.

Finally, remember that there is a fundamental difference between apologies and amends. We apologize all the time…and then go back to our same old broken behavior. If you are sincere, you are going to tell another person that, not only are you sorry for your mistakes, you are willing to make up for them and do the work so that they won't happen again.

CHAPTER SEVEN
PERSEVERANCE

We're awfully busy, aren't we? Busy with our work, busy with our social lives…just generally too busy to be happy. The hard truth is that it takes time to change life-long habits. You're going to continue to make little messes when you get greedy or lazy again; yes, those broken behaviors reappear. The difference is that you're going to recognize, in the moment, that you're at least partly responsible and that you don't want to be a victim anymore.

If you're like me, you want to just wrap things up and move on. Well, the bad news is that spiritual sickness (which is what we're really talking about here) takes a lifetime of treatment. The good news is that you will get better and better at dealing quickly and effectively with your broken behaviors.

Let's talk about this idea of spiritual sickness for a minute. Alcoholics and addicts of all stripes look at

129

their affliction as a disease. You may not be an alcoholic or an addict but your particular problem has still caused you a lot of pain. Why not try thinking of your behavior in the same way?

If you had some kind of chronic illness like asthma, you wouldn't be surprised or overly concerned about occasionally taking medicine when you had a flair-up, would you? Well, it's the same for those of us who need to use *The Principles* to deal with re-occurring everyday problems. Some of us have a worse case of broken behaviors and need more medication. Others can get by with low doses. But, if I were you, I'd give myself a break and take the "medicine" that this process represents. Why not feel better?

I believe that, if you're completely honest with yourself, you will have to admit that whatever problem brought you to *The Principles* is not a one-time occurrence. It's been with you for a long time, sneaking back into your life just when you thought you had a handle on it. Those of us who have problems in love don't just have one bad relationship – we repeat the same bad relationship over and over. Others who find work challenging don't struggle in just one job – their entire careers are filled with fear, anger, and

130

disappointment. Having a problem with your kids? Didn't your parents have the same problem with you? The reason is that the same spiritual problems fuel whole lifetimes of bad decisions.

It sounds like an awful lot of work to change, doesn't it? I have found it to be a lot of work but with an unexpected reward. When I work on problems of love or dating, my career improves. When I see my part in difficult family situations, I take better care of my health and exercise more. What I am saying here is that all of our problems are like a giant tree's vast root system. What goes into one root affects the whole tree, for better or worse. If I let poison seep into the roots around my career, eventually that toxin will reach the part of the tree where love or parenting grows. But if I give healthy spiritual nutrition to any part of the tree, all of it will flourish.

Yes, this is a lifetime of work. Yes, it will give you a life worth living.

Helen Perseveres With Dating

Helen could hardly believe that she had been dating Ed (formerly known as the hated Surfer) for three months. Since their little talk on the phone, Ed had called her consistently, or she called him. No big deal, no games. So Helen had a catch on her hands – hunky, sweet, and he even had a decent business going with his board shop.

But then, old "superficial, not ready for commitment" Helen started to come back. She found herself wondering about all those fantastic guys who were still out there waiting for her. She started to notice that Ed's hair was pretty much gone at 30. She even went to dinner with a Hollywood agent!

Fortunately for Helen, she'd gotten in the habit of being honest with her gal pals who were also using *The Principles*. These girls, who had previously co-signed her B.S., suddenly didn't want to hear her moaning about love.

When Helen called to complain that she didn't want to be tied-down, Tammy sweetly said, "Oh, honey, I think this pity party is cancelled." *Click!*

When Helen called to report on her date with the hot TV packaging agent (who might be a little bit

132

unavailable because he didn't return her calls), Lisa suggested, "Sounds great. Let me know how that turns out for you." *Click!*

In desperation, Helen even called her mom looking for a little sympathy for her wishy-washy ways. Helen gasped when her mother cooed, "Darling, you're no spring chicken. Isn't it about time to grow-up?"

Well, Helen had to break out the Responsibility Worksheet and then say a little prayer to her father.

Turns out there's nothing to run from...certainly not Ed.

Tom Perseveres With Work

Strangely, Tom and his ex-boss had become buddies since Tom got canned and then made amends. The guy even helped him line-up a new job, closer to home, which paid just as much as his old position.

Tom was doing great in his new position and hardly noticed traffic anymore. But then the old Tom started sneaking back little by little. His new boss (a woman, by the way) felt it necessary to sit Tom down and point out that he didn't take criticism very well. She even told Tom that he could be a bit of a jerk and had better get his ego under control if he wanted to continue working as *her* employee.

"*Her* employee," Tom fumed as he drove home that night. Like it was *her* company. Like *her* experience qualified *her* for *her* job.

Tom called his ex-boss for advice, hoping that the guy would commiserate with him. Instead, he asked Tom a question, "Does any of this sound familiar to you, Tom?"

"You mean like when I was working with you?" Tom replied.

"Um, when you were working *for* me, Tom."

Uh oh, busted. Tom had a case of arrogance as persistent as poison ivy and it had come back with a vengeance. Tom had to spend some quiet time thinking back to all the times that arrogance had kicked him in the rear end.

The next day Tom went into work and didn't apologize to his boss. He just did a great job with no attitude and got over himself.

Marlene Perseveres With Parenting
The other day, Marlene heard herself talking in capitals again. "People don't UNDERSTAND that being a mother is a FULL TIME JOB. You don't get ANY

134

respect if you don't have a BIG CAREER. Mothers
DESERVE respect."

Marlene's sister listened to about ten minutes of
this tirade before she said, "Who are you trying to
convince, Mar? 'Cause you don't have to convince me.
I'm a stay-at-homer too, remember?"

Marlene sputtered, "That's WHY I thought YOU,
of all people, could see how hard this is!"

Marlene's sister put down her needle-point and
patted the sofa, "OK, hon, take your hand off the throttle
and sit down a minute." Marlene was uneasy but
decided to come in for a landing. Her sister took
Marlene's hand and said very gently, "You were not
sentenced to motherhood. It was your choice. If it's not
what you want, get a babysitter and go back to work."

Marlene had to admit that she may have
temporarily put away some of her broken behavior but
she'd done absolutely nothing else to change her life.
No wonder she was back to her old routine; she hadn't
changed her behavior.

Marlene was ashamed to tell her sister, "I feel
like I'm a bad mom if I go back to work."

Her sister had already returned to her
needlepoint but murmured, "You think you can be a

135

good mom when you're this unhappy? Kinda selfish not to go back to work if it makes you this nuts not to."

Bernie Perseveres With Dating
Bernie has been dating his on-line confidante, MatureMacho, for several months now. On lots of levels, it's been great. MatureMacho (aka Frank) is actually able to pay for his own dinner and couldn't be less interested in the entertainment industry. Frank even let slip that he might like to adopt a child, to which Bernie replied, "Little long in the tooth for that, don't you think?"

Bernie really, really likes everything about Frank...except for his age. Mid-50s looks like...well, mid-50s. Frank had described himself honestly; he was handsome, macho, had a little gut and hair in places Bernie never thought possible. In other words, he was a real guy.

Bernie found himself increasingly transfixed by the sight of the golden, hairless 20-somethings he saw at the gym. He liked the way he felt when would-be actors recognized him, whispered to one another, and made their way over to help him lift weights. He was so

136

intoxicated by their beauty that he felt drunk at the sight of these young gods.

Fortunately, Bernie was no longer under the impression that these guys saw him as anything other than a meal ticket. He also knew that his own self-hatred and childishness made him pursue these guys despite the heartache that came along with them.

Bernie went back to his father's grave last weekend. He didn't really pray but he read a list he'd written of what he wanted in a relationship. As he read the list to his father, he realized that, while unemployed muscle boys had few of the qualities he wanted, Frank had most of them.

Ashley Perseveres With Her Weight
Ashley had lost 20 pounds and been walking religiously when she jumped into a big pit of self-pity and fixed it with a cherry cheesecake and a bag of Doritos. "Why did I do it? Why am I such a loser?" she moaned.

When Ashley's mom called to see if she would be coming by for Sunday dinner, Ashley lashed out, "Do you think I can lose weight with all that stuff you fix? You don't think it's food unless it has a stick of butter in it!"

137

Ashley's mom seems to have gotten sick of being Ashley's punching bag because she responded calmly, "OK, dear. Then I guess you'd better stay at home and cook for yourself."

Ashley stewed for an hour and got halfway through a jar of peanut butter before she whipped out her feelings list and Responsibility Worksheet:

When mom cooks for me, I feel ashamed, guilty, ugly, repulsive, lonely, and sad. My part is that I'm still a childish brat who wants to blame everything on mommy.

Ashley ditched the rest of the Skippy Super-Crunchy and headed to the grocery store. She loaded her cart with a turkey, fresh veggies, olive oil, and fruit. When she showed up at her mother's house with the bags, her mother didn't bat an eyelash. She said, "I don't need any apologies from you, young lady. I intend to have a manicure and let you cook."

Ashley kissed her mother, got to work making a healthy meal, and felt better than she had in years.

To Sum Up About Perseverance

I wonder sometimes what would happen if I became the perfect, spiritually-evolved being that I fantasize about. I'd probably just disappear in a big puff of smoke. Very gradually, I'm starting to realize that the Principles are about the journey, not the destination. If I am making progress, however slowly, I really don't have to worry about my mistakes along the way.

The problem comes when I get lazy or defensive. In that state, I decide that I've done enough work on myself and "it's time for all these other people to step up to the plate." Well, they may or may not. Even when I'm not the problem, I can be the solution.

What's more, if I am honest about continuing to make mistakes, I can probably help some other people working on similar problems. Who wants to hang out with Mr. Perfect? It's intimidating and, let's face it, even a little boring. No, I'd much rather be with other flawed people who are trying as best they can. That inspires me.

Self-pity can be a killer when we get to this stage in our spiritual journey because it seems like it takes so much work just to be happy. But what I often

139

forget is how truly unhappy I once was. All I need to do is sit quietly and look at the Surrender Worksheet to see what brought me to this process and how far I've come. In that moment, self-pity disappears (along with laziness, defensiveness, and a big heap of fear) because I know that I'm happier than I was and can see the benefit of persevering on this path.

Great! So I'm going to be doing this my whole life?

Yes, *if* you really want to be happy. And no one can convince you whether or not doing the work to be happy is worth it or not. It's up to you.

Tips on Perseverance

- Clean up your messes (caused by going back to broken behaviors) quickly. The sooner you clean it up, the easier it is. Imagine a dirty dinner plate – is it is easier to wash it right away or let the food get dry and crusty?
- Avoid self-pity and self-obsession like the plague.
- Continue to practice contrary action.
- Be patient with yourself and expect to make mistakes.
- Remember where you were emotionally and spiritually when you started this process and give yourself credit for the progress you've made.

Mantra
My mistakes are opportunities for humility and growth.

Perseverance Worksheet

What are the situations that take me back to my old broken behaviors?

_____

_____

_____

_____

_____

What are the patterns I see in my behavior?

_____

_____

_____

_____

_____

While working on *The Principles*, these are the problems that I have not yet addressed or things that I could have done better.

_____

_____

_____

_____

_____

Tool – Making Goals

We spend a lot of time looking at our faults in this process but we also have to give ourselves goals to continue moving forward. It is your decision but I prefer goals that are reasonable and specific. When making goals, I ask my Higher Power to guide me and to give me dreams that will not be harmful to me or those I love. In other words, if my dream were to be successful in business, I would hope that my Higher Power would protect me from obtaining a job that was so consuming that it would cause me to neglect my family.

And be honest with yourself when making goals; they're your goals, after all. If you are working on love and dating, what are the specific qualities you are looking for in a mate? Honestly. Do they have to have a hot bod or simply be healthy and in reasonable shape? Do they need to have stable finances or do you want them to be mega-successful? What is your goal?

If your career is the issue that has brought you to *The Principles*, what kind of work life do you want to achieve? Really. Do you want to just have a good job or do you need to be the boss? Is your salary more important or your home life?

143

Maybe parenting concerns brought you to *The Principles*. What kind of relationship do you want with your children? Tell the truth. Do you want your children to be the central focus of your life or balanced with other activities? Do you want your children to be independent or is it more important that they do things your way?

There are no right answers. These are *your* hopes and dreams. All you need to do is to be honest. After that, it's between you and your God.

CHAPTER EIGHT
SPIRITUALITY

Here's a quick test for you. Look at the last word on the previous page. How do you feel when you read it – uncomfortable or comforted, angry or serene, judgmental or compassionate?

There is nothing like the word *God* to bring up strong emotions. Even though I have lived a spiritual life for some time, I still have an uneasy feeling when I talk about God, as if I will be mistaken for a fundamentalist or perceived as somehow uncool. The word itself is the problem because I am absolutely sure in my belief that there is some kind of organizing, loving force in the universe that wants me to be happy. But when I publicly term that force God, suddenly I feel ashamed.

So both for myself and for you, I have sprinkled the word God throughout this book along with phrases like Higher Power, Nature, and "whatever you believe in." I think we can desensitize ourselves to the embarrassment so many of us feel about spirituality through using these terms publicly.

Because organized religion is so polarizing, it is a continual struggle to remind people that spirituality is different than religion because it is completely personal. If you've come this far in *The Principles*, then you already know on some level, from your own experience, that faith in a power greater than you can lift you out of victim-hood and propel you into a healthier, happier life.

Fear is the one human shortcoming that drives our bad behavior more than any other. And there's no denying that there is much to be afraid of in modern life. But how do we continue to grow and avoid having fear take us back to our old problems? You need to find at least some small way to keep a Higher Power (or God, if you will) in your life. Paths of spiritual seeking are as different as our conceptions of God. For some, it might be learning to meditate or taking time to pray. For others, it may be walking on the beach and remembering that something, somewhere, helped us with a problem that we once believed to be unsolvable.

Although paths of spiritual exploration may be very different, they all have the same destination: gratitude. When I am spiritually connected, I am much

146

more likely to feel grateful for everything I have rather than to waste my days worrying about what I still want.

Remember that this Principle is called *spirituality*, not religion. For those of you who are uncomfortable with religion, there is absolutely no reason you cannot seek spiritually in your own, individual way. And for those who are religious, spiritual practices such as meditation and peaceful walks in nature can only deepen your religious beliefs.

Our characters will give us some different examples of spiritual paths and I would like you to note a few things in their stories – most importantly, that these stories all involve the characters *taking action*. Like everything else in *The Principles*, spirituality requires action. To sit down to meditate is action, to walk in nature is action, to go to church or synagogue or temple or mosque is action. As modern culture is so action-oriented, perhaps it will be easier for you to include spirituality in your daily life is you think of it as being as action-oriented as going to the gym or rigorously pursuing your career. Spirituality yields just as many, if not more, results as these other activities.

Helen Gets Spiritual

The first time Helen went surfing, it was pretty much to humor Ed. Also she knew she looked pretty hot in a wet suit. But there was something about the depth and power of the water...

Within a few months, Helen was surfing solo. She would catch a wave or two but mostly she just floated on her board and felt peaceful for the first time in her life. Helen had spent so many years trying to manipulate and scheme that she had forgotten how great it was to totally let go.

"How'd I get here?" Helen wondered on a particularly magnificent morning in Malibu as the waves gently lifted her up and then softly slid out from underneath her. The neurotic, self-obsessed brat from Manhattan was floating in the Pacific Ocean, completely at ease with herself. She knew that, if Ed left her, she would be fine. If she lost her job, she would be fine. If she got wrinkled and old and fat, she'd be (mostly) fine.

Helen had perhaps been to church three times in her entire life. It wasn't like her parents had been dismissive of religion; it just wasn't their thing. But on fine California days, with the sounds of seagulls and crashing waves surrounding her, Helen knew that there

148

was a plan to the world. She would draw in a deep, deep breath and close her eyes as she whispered, "Thank you, God. Thank you for this life."

Tom Gets Spiritual

Tom is a churchgoer. He likes the rituals, the prayers, and the music. Tom likes knowing that he is part of a tradition that stretches back hundreds of years.

One of the things that Tom likes about going to church is meeting people. Until recently, he didn't realize how lonely he'd become. Completely focused on work, Tom's friends had dropped away. Angry and resentful, Tom hadn't been such a great friend anyway. But, gradually, he's become a more appealing guy and started participating in the social part of church life. Tom has often felt God as strongly during a church car wash or softball game as during the services. At those events, he feels a part of something.

In addition to the set prayers, Tom prays informally all through the day. At first he thought it was weird but he found that prayer worked. When he wants to scream at his boss, Tom goes outside for a moment, looks up at the sky and pleads, "Please help me be the person you want me to be." When Tom stands in line at

149

the grocery store and wants to tell off the person who decides to write a check instead of using a debit card, he takes a deep breath instead and remembers, "I'm fine. I'm not alone anymore."

A lot of Tom's spiritual life takes place in church but he has found that helping other people has brought him the greatest rewards. More about that in the final chapter of *The Principles*.

Marlene Gets Spiritual

Marlene went back to work part-time recently at a small law firm in her town. Instead of feeling overwhelmed with both her daughter and work, Marlene finds she has more energy and peace than she's known in years. But there are days when she feels drained and starts to worry, "Did I make the right decision? Is my daughter getting what she needs?"

Not having a lot of spare time, Marlene needed to find a spiritual practice that could fit into her schedule. Fortunately, there is a lunchtime yoga class at the local community center just around the corner from her office. Several times a week, Marlene heads out of the office with a gym bag and works on her Downward Dog, Cobra and Pigeon Pose for an hour.

There are no gurus in her small town yoga class, just a middle-aged woman who leads the class as best she can. But it is spiritual even without all the big city yoga studio trappings.

Marlene is getting a tighter tummy and increased flexibility during yoga but the more important benefits are internal. At first, she was very judgmental about the teacher's New Age mottos like "Trust yourself," and "Let yourself believe that, in this moment, you have everything you need."

But after a few weeks, Marlene actually *was* trusting herself. She began to know intuitively when her daughter needed more attention and when she could simply let go, knowing everything was OK.

Several classes later, Marlene was lying in the cool, dark room at the end of class when she had a sensation that was entirely new. Tears ran down her face as she thought, "Right here, right now, everything is just fine."

Marlene plans to add a weekend yoga class to her schedule and she doesn't feel in the least bit selfish about taking the time to do so. Her spirituality has become another part of being a good mom.

Bernie Gets Spiritual

As you've seen, Bernie has never shied away from spiritual practices. But, in truth, they were mostly ways to pick up guys. Bernie only took yoga from the hunky teacher, he only went to all-male sweat lodges, and his hikes were always on trails that had "other attractions."

Bernie has returned to a lot of those same activities and is a little defensive about his buffet approach to spirituality. "Hey, what can I tell you? I'm a seeker." But Bernie doesn't need to be embarrassed by his spiritual *smorgasbord*. In fact, he's exactly right – to seek is the most important part of the process. As we change, our spiritual needs change with us. There's nothing wrong with letting your spiritual activities evolve.

Bernie has even added church to his roster of activities. He found the local Metropolitan Community Church, with a gay congregation who seemed more interested in supporting each other than cruising.

The other new element in Bernie's journey is that he has invited his boyfriend (yes, they made it official) Frank to join him. Before, the idea of having a serious conversation with someone he was dating seemed entirely beside the point. But Bernie is beginning to realize that having a spiritual connection with a man is nearly as important to him as having a sexual connection.

Several days a week, Frank and Bernie meet at sunset and hike to the top of the Hollywood Hills. When they reach the top, they have a little ritual of holding hands as the sun sets. Before they start back down the trail, Bernie always thinks of his father and says silently, "Thank you."

Ashley Gets Spiritual

Ashley found God while doing a double-reverse turn in step aerobics class. Really. Having spent her entire life dreading physical exercise, Ashley was astounded to find that she absolutely loves it. She was even more amazed when she discovered that exercise was a spiritual practice for her.

Ashley feels *connected* in sweaty spinning classes with the music pounding, surrounded by other students, with the teacher yelling, "Come on! Push yourself!" She feels *wonder* as she pounds along the running path with the sun blazing and the wind blowing. And Ashley feels *love* enveloped in the warm quiet peace of the yoga studio.

153

But it was in step class that she finally realized that she had found her version of God. For months, she had been taking the most advanced step class she could find in her area. It was like a Vegas show with its intricate routines and carefully mixed music. She had started in the back of the class, mortified by her stumbling performance. But she didn't give up. For the first time in her life, Ashley didn't give up. Week by week, she moved forward in the room until she found herself standing next to the instructor in the front row. One day, the instructor, who Ashley had always been painfully shy with, winked at her and said, "Let's go, girl."

On that day, Ashley lost herself in the music and stopped thinking about the impossibly complicated series of steps. As she swung toward the back of the room in a double-reverse turn, she thought, "My God, I've never been happier in my whole life."

Ashley is one lucky girl because her spiritual life also heals her physical body.

To sum up about spirituality…

Many people who would benefit from using *The Principles* in daily life instead rebel against them because they confuse spirituality for religion. The benefit of using *The Principles* is that you can construct your own spiritual path, free from religious baggage. Whether or not you are religious, you can turn over your problems, whatever they may be, to a power greater than yourself rather than trying to control everything yourself.

Spend an afternoon walking along the beach, gazing out at the constantly moving ocean. Can you feel the water's depth and power, the inevitability of its waves as they crash on the shore? That is a spiritual experience connecting you to a power greater than yourself. That experience is equally available to a Catholic, a Jew, a Muslim, and an agnostic.

Mantra
I give my life to a power greater than myself and trust that I am cared for, loved, and safe.

155

Tips on Spirituality

- Remember that religion and spirituality are not necessarily the same.
- Think outside the box when developing spiritual activities.
- Don't worry if you don't always feel spiritually connected. No one does.
- Develop friendships while practicing spiritual activities.

Spirituality Worksheet

These are the activities that help me feel connected to my Higher Power or God:

_____

_____

_____

_____

_____

_____

These are my doubts about spirituality:

_____

_____

_____

_____

_____

I commit to doing these activities weekly to remain spiritually fit:

_____

_____

_____

_____

CHAPTER NINE
HELPING OTHERS

You've been on a long journey and, hopefully, it has changed you. Your inclination might be to kick back and enjoy the benefits of a life not ruled by the problems that initially brought you to *The Principles*. That would be a mistake.

The last Principle is the most powerful in terms of maintaining your spiritual health. It has the ability to vanquish self-pity and self-obsession. It builds self-esteem where before there was only self-loathing. And I absolutely guarantee that this Principle will mean that you are never lonely again. The last Principle is *Helping Others*.

The idea of helping others is so powerful that it is at the center of many spiritual belief systems. Nearly all churches have charitable programs as part of their structure. In the Hindu tradition of Seva, one of the routes to illumination is *charya*, or selfless service. And, of course, 12-step programs believe that service to others is the key to continued sobriety.

As with all the other Principles, your practice of helping others will be individual. But I am confident that you will never feel better about yourself than when you are helping another person. Your might volunteer at a charity or help someone who is homeless. You might even end up helping some of the people you used to resent but have become close to through using *The Principles.*

Or your service might be something as small as being compassionate when someone says to you, "I have this problem and it's driving me crazy." You can just nod and say, "I know. Me too."

Helen Helps

Helen has never been a joiner and she doesn't have a maternal bone in her body. Or so she thought...

Helen was shocked when a friend who works in a drop-in center for troubled teens suggested that she volunteer. And Helen was even more shocked when she heard herself say, "Yeah, I've been wanting to do something like that."

The shelter asked Helen to mentor a teenage girl named Amy who came from an abusive family. Helen's responsibility involved nothing more than hanging out with this girl every Saturday afternoon for two or three hours.

The first Saturday was predictably awkward as the two walked around the city window-shopping and then ate lunch. When the time came for Helen to drop Amy back at the center, she felt the day had been a miserable failure. It was like she'd been on a bad date.

Then a miracle happened. As Amy was getting out of the car, she asked Helen if they could meet again the next Saturday. Perhaps for the first time in her entire life, Helen felt real pride as she casually told Amy, "Sure. No problem."

160

Helen hasn't gotten married yet. She's dating and surfing. But Helen has discovered an amazing fact. As long as she's takes actions that make her happy and proud, finding a man doesn't have to be the ultimate goal. When Helen shows up for Amy, she feels a happiness that she has never gotten from a relationship. So Helen still wants to find Mr. Right…but she's not in such a hurry anymore because life's pretty darn good as it is.

Tom Helps

Tom's ex-boss got sick and he's not likely to get any better. Weirdly, the guy called Tom to ask for help. It's not a big deal but sometimes the guy needs somebody to fix stuff around the house when he's not feeling up to it. Tom runs to the grocery store for him on weekends. Totally not a big deal…except that it has changed Tom's life.

Every time that Tom shows up for his ex-boss, he feels the rage and arrogance drain from him like water out of a sink. Once the guy actually needed somebody to pick him up at the hospital. So there was Tom, walking into the hospital room of the man he used

161

to hate more than anybody in the world. And that guy was so happy to see Tom, so grateful for his help. That man, who Tom was absolutely sure was the worst person in the world, had somehow become Tom's friend.

Tom got it. Anytime that he started to feel the old anger start to come back, he found a way to help somebody. He showed up at the church to volunteer. He called up his ex-wife to see if she needed anything. Just about anything that Tom could do to focus on another person helped him to feel better about himself.

Tom goes to his job now and doesn't feel like every task is an insult. He hasn't had a run-in with his boss in ages. Sometimes Tom can't even remember what he was so mad about a few months ago.

Marlene Helps

Marlene went back to work to become a soccer mom. Before she went back to work, Marlene felt like every minute of every day was spoken for. Strangely, now that she's back at work and spends less time obsessing about making life perfect, there is a lot more time for things she actually enjoys.

162

And one of the things Marlene enjoys the most is volunteering as a soccer coach at her daughter's school. The kids are so young that they can barely kick the ball in the right direction, let alone score a goal. As Marlene said one day to an irate parent, "Winning is SO not the point."

When Marlene's daughter crawls in the car completely covered in mud, Marlene is in heaven. When the kids cry and don't want to play, Marlene loves giving pep talks. When Marlene's husband doesn't want to get up on a Saturday for the game, Marlene hauls him out of bed anyway.

It's not that Marlene finds it so easy to be a working mom. There are plenty of nights that she's dead tired and her daughter is cranky and she realizes that she hasn't had sex with her husband in weeks. But Marlene's days are now filled with activity. She doesn't have time to think about herself. If she thinks about how she can be as helpful as possible at work, she doesn't get competitive with the other lawyers. If she keeps focused on helping all the kids at soccer, she doesn't mind when her daughter sits down and refuses to play. When Marlene offers to babysit for her sister, all those years of petty jealousy just wash away.

Bernie Helps

Bernie had to learn that other gay men were good for something other than sexual pleasure. This may not seem a very difficult concept for most but it had really never occurred to Bernie that he could admire other gay men without wanting to have sex with them.

Bernie isn't one for subtlety. "Where can I meet gay men who I absolutely won't want to have sex with? It's impossible!" The answer came to him when he received an invitation for an event benefiting a gay and lesbian retirement home.

Although the very concept of a gay old age home was the most horrifying thing Bernie could think of, he went to the benefit and later signed up to be a volunteer there. His job was just to go into people's rooms and talk to them. Instead, he took along a huge pile of *Vogue* and *Men's Health* magazines on his first day and handed them out to the old guys with only a few words. It was horrible! Bernie rushed into the last room, trying not to burst into tears.

In that last room, Bernie quickly deposited a magazine in front of a rather dapper old codger in a bow tie and turned to walk away. The man grabbed Bernie's

164

hand. "You're a busy one, aren't ya? Just sit down here for a minute."

Bernie uneasily sat down next to the man whose name turned out to be Dean. Dean was pushing 90 and had lost his partner a few years back. The two of them had been together for nearly 50 years. "50 years?" Bernie whispered incredulously. "Tell me."

Turns out that Bernie and Dean both got a lot out of Bernie's volunteer efforts. Dean got to tell his life story one more time and Bernie got to find out that gay life could be different than he ever thought.

Ashley Helps

Ashley has been working at Camp Fit for a few months now. Camp Fit helps overweight kids lose weight through a program of exercise, healthy eating, and therapy. It also gives the kids a safe place to talk about their feelings for the first time. Ashley thinks sometimes that she should be paying Camp Fit for the opportunity to work there.

Most of the counselors were also overweight as children. During the nightly rap sessions, counselors talk about their own experiences growing up heavy and then encourage the kids to share their stories. The first few times that Ashley tried to talk she spent most of the time weeping and the kids comforted her. Now, though, Ashley can just tell her story. Sometimes she even brings along her Feelings List to tell the kids what it was like back when she was alone and hopeless…because it's been a long time since she felt that way.

What amazes Ashley is that she gets so much comfort out of being around people with the same problem. Instead of being depressing, it inspires her to keep up with her own program of exercise and healthy eating. When she wants to plunge back into self-pity or throw a hissy fit by eating a package of Twinkies, she thinks of the kids. The idea of being a role model for them is a powerful appetite suppressant for Ashley.

Ashley is not rail thin. She's always going to be a curvy girl. But she can actually look in the mirror now and she who she really is – a good person. When she gets in a bad place, she thinks of the kids of Camp Fit. Then she takes the love and compassion she feels for them, and gives it back to herself.

To sum up about helping others…

My suggestion to you is to spend as little time thinking about yourself as possible. You've done the hard work of facing your problem, taking responsibility for it, and making up for your shortcomings. Now you want to fight the self-obsession that feeds your broken behaviors. When you are focused on helping others, it is very difficult to plunge back into that old pool of self-pity.

Helping others is, in a way, selfish. You will probably get more out of it than the people you help. But I think that kind of selfishness is just fine. The world will benefit and so will you.

With all my heart, I encourage you to find a way to give back to others. I know the happiness it has brought me and I hope that you will be able to experience this purest of all joys.

Volunteer work is depressing! I feel great now and I don't want to ruin the mood.

You're cheating yourself with that attitude. Why do you think so many rich, talented, beautiful people are

167

miserable? They have too much time to obsess about their petty little problems. Helping others is going to be the least depressing thing you've ever done. Promise.

Mantra

Today I will focus on how I can help others. In helping them, I help myself.

Worksheet – Helping Others

These are five opportunities to help others:

_____

_____

_____

_____

Every week I commit to do the following to help others:

_____

_____

_____

_____

When I help others, I feel (use the Feelings List):

_____

_____

_____

_____

Compare your feelings of *helping others* to your feelings of *surrender* in Chapter One. Which set of feelings would you rather have?

Tool – Selfless Service

Many of us enjoy supporting charities by attending glamorous benefits where star entertainers perform or we get to rub elbows with those who might later help us in business. These events do a great deal to support a range of worthy organizations and I absolutely encourage you to attend them if you can afford to do so.

But, in *The Principles*, we're looking for opportunities where you can help others and, in return, help yourself. In my experience, you will get the most spiritual benefit out of *selflessly* helping others. That means I need to perform my volunteer efforts with no agenda. Other than raising my own self-esteem, I expect nothing in return. If my volunteering keeps me from returning to broken behaviors or wallowing in self-pity, I don't need a glittering evening of stars. The feelings I get are reward enough.

The same holds true when helping an individual. Inevitably, when I have chosen to help someone who I thought could prove useful to me later, it turned out to be a disaster. I ended up resenting the very person I wanted to help.

So, again, party on when you have the itch to attend one of those glitzy benefits. But find something a little more humble, even anonymous, when you are looking for the spiritual reward that comes from helping others.

CHAPTER TEN
WHY THE PRINCIPLES?

It seems there is a self-help program for every problem in the world. There are gurus and preachers eager to give you the answers you seek. And therapy has become an accepted part of American life rather than something reserved for the rich and neurotic. So why should you follow *The Principles*?

When I decided to write about *The Principles*, I wanted to gather together some of the great lessons offered by the world's religions as well as spiritual programs such as the 12-steps. It always seemed to me that people without very severe, life threatening problems were unlikely to use such tools because they believed them to be reserved for those who were either very spiritual or very sick.

The fact is that ideas such as surrender, honesty, humility, and responsibility are by their very nature universal and need not be limited to any particular religion or spiritual organization. To limit

172

access to these ideas and the relief they can bring would be the ultimate act of selfishness. My hope is that *The Principles* will begin to help normal people move toward lives that are both practical and spiritual.

An interesting exercise is to apply *The Principles* to the news of the world. Each day as I watch TV, read news on-line, or peruse the papers, I think of *The Principles*. Earlier in life, I found the news depressing but didn't understand why. Now I know that my frustration with politics, for example, is that political figures so seldom practice responsibility and honesty. Once you have become committed to using *The Principles* in daily life, you are bound to find that you have less interest in celebrities wallowing in their "problems" and other media coverage that does not involve people taking responsibility for their lives and trying to change.

I also find myself impatient with much of the bluster that has become a part of American culture. To my mind, we would do better to surrender to the fact that we face extensive problems, and begin to work on them. Instead, we seem like the proverbial ostrich with its head in the sand.

I'm sure that your political views will differ from mine even if we agree on the value of *The Principles*.

However, I have to believe that we could at least have a productive discussion about what can be done to alleviate suffering and promote peace. Our interpretations of how *The Principles* are either followed or abandoned in the world will be as various as our individual beliefs in a Higher Power. But I believe *The Principles* at least allow us to speak a common language about integrity, ethics, and the common good.

On the other hand…there is a danger to writing about politics and current events using the lens of *The Principles*. The danger is that my political views, however sound I believe them to be, can turn off others who would benefit from using *The Principles*. That is why, in this book, I have tried to avoid controversy. The characters I created to illustrate *The Principles* here are diverse – straight and gay, men and women, married and single, rich and working class, urban and rural – in hopes that nearly anyone can relate.

Finally, I want you to make this book yours by reinterpreting it as you wish. It is my belief that each spiritual journey is unique. There may be tools here that are useful for discovering your path but I hope you won't feel constrained to use them.

This belief was reinforced while I was researching *The Principles*. I contacted Alcoholics

174

Anonymous World Services to ask if A.A. had ever created an official list of spiritual principles to be used in 12-step work. The very nice person I spoke with explained to me that A.A. had intentionally never codified the principles because they believed every spiritual path should be individual. Unlike the steps and traditions of A.A., the program's principles, while much discussed, have never been formalized.

So you may well find that there are Principles that you think should be included here, which are not. Add them! Think of ways to make them present in your life! I can imagine, for example, that kindness and compassion should be included in *The Principles*. Of course, I find those qualities in Principles such as forgiveness and helping others. But if you want to create your own set of Principles, I hope you will do so.

I am not a moral authority. *The Principles* reflects my life and the lessons I have learned. As you make this journey yourself, you will develop your own ideas and pass them along to others. That is the great joy of the Principles and ultimately their greatest endorsement – the ways in which they are implemented in our lives continually changes and evolves. And if the Principles change, why can't we?

TOOL KIT
FEELINGS LIST

abandoned	alert	astonished	bored
absent-minded	alive	astounded	bossy
absorbed	alluring	attached	bothered
accepted	almighty	attractive	bottled up
aching	aloof	avid	boxed in
achy	ambitious	awed	brave
active	ambivalent	awkward	breathless
actualized	amused	-----------------	brisk
adamant	angry	bad	broken up
adaptable	annoyed	badgered	bruised
adequate	anxious	battered	bubbly
adored	apathetic	beautiful	buoyant
adventurous	appalled	beaten	burdened
affected	appealing	belligerent	------------------
affectionate	appreciative	bereaved	caged
afflicted	apprehensive	betrayed	callous
afraid	apologetic	bewildered	calm
aggravated	ardent	bitchy	capable
aggressive	argumentative	bitter	captivated
agonized	aroused	blah	carefree
agreeable	arrogant	blissful	careless
aglow	artistic	boastful	caring
agony	ashamed	boiling	cautious
alarmed	assertive	bold	certain

176

challenged	conflicted	deceitful	dignified
changeable	confused	deceived	diminished
charmed	conspicuous	defeated	dirty
cheated	conscientious	defensive	disappointed
cheerful	conservative	deflated	disapproving
cheery	considerate	degraded	disbelieving
cherished	consumed	dejected	discontented
childish	contemptuous	delighted	discouraged
choked-up	contented	demanding	discreet
civilized	contrite	demeaned	disdain
clear	conventional	demoralized	disgraced
clever	cool	demure	disgusted
close	cooperative	dependable	dismal
closed	cornered	dependent	dismayed
coarse	courageous	depressed	disorderly
cold	cowardly	deprived	disorganized
combative	crabby	deserted	dissatisfied
comfortable	cranky	desirous	distasteful
common	crappy	despair	distracted
competent	crazy	desperate	distraught
competitive	cross	despondent	distressed
compassion	cruel	desolate	distrustful
complacent	crushed	destroyed	disturbed
complaining	cuddly	destructive	divided
complete	curious	determined	dominant
concentrating	cynical	devastated	dominated
concerned	------------------	devoted	domineering
condemned	damned	different	doomed
confident	daring	diffident	doubtful

177

down	envious	foresighted	gleeful
drained	evasive	forgetful	gloomy
dreadful	evil	forgiving	glowing
dreary	exasperated	forlorn	good
dubious	excited	formal	grateful
dull	exhausted	forsaken	gratified
-----------------	exhilarated	fortunate	greedy
eager	exposed	forward	grief
earnest	exuberant	frank	grieving
eavesdropping	-----------------	frantic	grim
ecstatic	fair	free	groovy
edgy	falling apart	friendly	grouchy
effeminate	fantastic	frightened	grumpy
efficient	fascinated	frisky	guarded
egotistical	fatherly	frivolous	guilty
elated	fawning	frozen	gullible
electrified	fear	frustrated	gutless
embarrassed	fearful	full	-----------------
emotional	fearless	fuming	happy
empathic	feminine	funny	hard
empty	festive	furious	hard-headed
enchanted	fidgety	fussy	hardy
encouraged	firm	-----------------	hasty
energetic	flat	generous	hassled
enervated	flattered	gentle	hate
engrossed	floating	genuine	hateful
enraged	flustered	giddy	headstrong
enterprising	foolish	giving	heartbroken
enthusiastic	forceful	glad	heavenly

178

heavy	idiotic	innocent	judged
helpful	ignorant	inquiring	jumpy
helpless	ignored	inquisitive	------------------
hemmed in	ill-at-ease	inspired	keen
heroic	imaginative	insecure	keyed up
hesitant	immature	insignificant	kinky
high	immobilized	insulted	kind
hilarious	immortal	intelligent	------------------
hollow	impatient	intent	laconic
homesick	important	interested	lazy
honest	imposed upon	intimate	lecherous
honored	impotent	intimidated	left out
hopeful	impressed	intolerant	leisurely
hopeless	impulsive	intrigued	let down
horrible	incompetent	inventive	licentious
horrified	incomplete	involved	light
hostile	indecisive	irate	lighthearted
humble	independent	irked	little
humiliated	indifferent	irresponsible	lively
humorless	indignant	irritable	loaded
humorous	industrious	irritated	logical
hungover	infantile	isolated	lonely
hurried	infatuated	------------------	longing
hurt	inflamed	jammed up	loose
hyper	informal	jealous	loud
hypocritical	infuriated	jittery	lovestruck
hysterical	ingenious	jolly	loving
------------------	inhibited	joyous	low
idealistic	injured	jubilant	loyal

179

lustful	nervous	pained	positive
-----------------	nice	pampered	potent
mad	noisy	panic	powerful
malicious	nostalgic	panicky	powerless
masculine	numb	paranoid	praiseworthy
mature	nutty	parsimonious	precarious
maudlin	-----------------	paralyzed	precise
mean	obliging	passionate	prejudged
meditative	obnoxious	pathetic	preoccupied
meek	obsessed	patient	pressured
merry	obstinate	peaceful	pretty
melancholy	odd	peculiar	prim
mild	offended	peeved	prissy
miscellaneous	omnipotent	perplexed	progressive
mischievous	open	persecuted	proud
miserable	on edge	persistent	prudish
mixed up	opposed	pessimistic	pulled apart
modest	optimistic	petrified	put down
moody	organized	pitiful	puzzled
motherly	out of control	pity	-----------------
mournful	out-of-sorts	pissed	quarrelsome
mystical	outraged	phony	queasy
mystified	outspoken	physical	queer
-----------------	outgoing	played out	questioning
nasty	overburdened	playful	quiet
natural	overjoyed	pleasant	-----------------
naughty	overwhelmed	pleased	rational
nauseated	-----------------	poised	rattled
negative	pain	polished	realistic

180

reasonable	rotten	sharp	soothed
reassured	rude	shattered	sophisticated
rebellious	ruined	sheepish	sorrowful
reckless	-----------------	shiftless	sorry
reflective	sad	shocked	sparkling
refreshed	safe	shook up	special
regretful	sarcastic	show-off	spineless
rejected	sated	shrewd	spiteful
relaxed	satisfied	shy	spontaneous
reliable	scared	sickened	spunky
relieved	screwed (up)	silent	squelched
remorseful	secure	silly	stable
renewed	seductive	simple	startled
repulsed	self-centered	sincere	starved
resentful	self-conscious	skeptical	steady
reserved	self-confident	skittish	stern
resourceful	selfish	slick	stifled
respected	sensitive	slow	stimulated
responsible	sentimental	sluggish	stiff
responsive	separate	sly	stingy
restful	serene	small	strained
restless	serious	smothered	strangled
reverent	servile	smug	stretched
revengeful	settled	sneaky	strong
revived	severe	snobbish	strung out
rewarded	sexy	sociable	stubborn
righteous	shaky	soft	stuffed
rigid	shallow	solemn	stupid
robbed	shameful	somber	stunned

181

stupefied
subdued
submissive
suffering
suffocated
sulky
sullen
superstitious
sure
surly
surprised
suspicious
sweaty
sweet
sympathetic
----
talkative
taut
tearful
tempted
tenacious
tender
tense
tentative
terrible
terrified
terrific
thankless
thankful

thoughtful
threatened
thrilled
thwarted
tickled
tight
timid
tired
together
tolerant
torn
tormented
tortured
touched
touchy
tough
tragic
trapped
tricked
troubled
trusting
turned on
two-faced
----
ugly
unaffected
unambitious
unassuming
unbelieving

uncertain
undecided
undependable
uncomfortable
understanding
uneasy
unexcitable
unfriendly
unhappy
uninhibited
unimportant
unintelligent
unkind
unsettled
unscrupulous
unstable
upset
uptight
used
useful
useless
----
vacant
valued
vehement
vindictive
violent
vital
vivacious

vulnerable
----
warm
wary
wasted
wavering
weak
weepy
whiny
whipped
wholesome
wicked
wiped out
wise
wishy-washy
withdrawn
witty
wonderful
worried
worthless
wrathful
----
yearning
----
zany
zealous

TOOL KIT
BROKEN BEHAVIORS

Arrogant

Bossy

Ashamed

Bossy

Cynical

Delusional

Dishonest

Envious

False pride

Fear confrontation

Financial fear

Gluttonous

Gossipy

Greedy

Hypocritical

Impatient

Inappropriate expectations

Intolerant

Jealous

Judgmental

Lack of compassion

183

Lazy

Low self-esteem

Lustful

Manipulative

Maudlin

Not listening to inner voice

Not living in today

Not trusting in God

Opportunistic

Oversensitive

People pleasing

Playing God

Retaliation

Self-destructive

Self-hating

Selfish

Self-pitying

Sloppy

Superficial

Superior

Unambitious

Ungrateful

Unreasonable expectations

Vain

Withdrawn

TOOL KIT
PRAYERS

Surrender

Once my world was huge and my mind was open to hope. Now, in this moment, I surrender to what my life has become. In my surrender, I will find hope once again. In my surrender, I will find the willingness to change.

Faith

I do not know you. But I ask you to reveal yourself. Show me some beauty or kindness in the world that will help me to believe that you exist and that my life can be happy once again.

Responsibility

I am no longer a victim, angry and afraid, lashing out at the world. I take my place in this world and take responsibility for the life I have created. In responsibility, there is hope. In hope, there is change.

Honesty

Not hiding in shame, not turning away with fear, not seeking the dark loneliness of difference, I reclaim my place in this world. I will join you by owning my truth, wherever it may take me.

Humility

I have carried this burden so long. Please help me to lay it down. Take it from me. I hand it to you in hopes of once again becoming the person you created. Today, I begin to change.

Forgiveness

My anger wraps around me like a flame, holding me back and pushing you away. I will put aside everything I believe about you and me. I cannot afford to throw you away or to be discarded myself. I need you in my life and I forgive you as you forgive me.

Perseverance

Help me never to be done. Help me never to arrive or to stop. Give me the maturity and strength to be imperfect but improving. Give me the hope and faith to always keep moving and growing.

Spirituality

Open my eyes to the wonder of the world around me. Open my mind to the wonder of the world I cannot see. Open my soul to the wonder of being connected and comforted and loved.

Helping Others

Free me from my self. In ways large and small, give me the opportunity to help others. Show me the happiness that comes from bringing comfort rather than pain, acceptance rather than judgment, and connection rather than isolation.

187

TOOL KIT
RESOURCES

The Principles is intended to help normal, non-addictive people with everyday problems. But there are many of us who have problems that require far more intensive help than this book is able to provide. If you need that kind of assistance, I encourage you to seek it without shame.

Although this book is inspired by the teachings of great religions and 12-step programs, it is not a substitute for religious organizations or addiction programs. If your problem is life threatening, please seek the help that is so readily available. If you are a person living with a severe mental, spiritual, or physical condition such as depression or chemical dependency, please use the contacts listed below or visit your local religious organization.

12-Step Programs

Alcoholics Anonymous

www.alcoholics-anonymous.org

Narcotics Anonymous

www.na.org

Crystal Meth Anonymous

www.crystalmeth.org

Overeaters Anonymous

www.oa.org

Sexual Compulsives Anonymous

www.sca-recovery.org

Hotlines

National Suicide Hotline
800-SUICIDE or 1-800-273-TALK

National Drug & Alcohol Treatment
800-662-HELP

National Domestic Violence Hotline

800-799-7233

National Child Abuse Hotline

800-4-A-CHILD

National Youth Crisis Hotline

800-HIT-HOME

National Adolescent Suicide Hotline

800-621-4000

National Runaway Hotline

800-621-4000

Panic Disorder Information Hotline

800- 64-PANIC